Lorraine Kelly's Scotland

LORRAINE KELLY'S
SCOTLAND

BANTAM PRESS

LONDON · TORONTO · SYDNEY · AUCKLAND · JOHANNESBURG

To Rosie, with love from Mum and Dad

CONTENTS

INTRODUCTION

OVER THE YEARS I HAVE BEEN lucky enough to travel all around Scotland. As a child my mum and dad took us on day trips from Glasgow to Loch Lomond and the Trossachs, and on holiday 'doon the watter' to the Ayrshire coast, and seaside towns like Largs, Saltcoats, Ayr, Prestwick and Troon, during the Glasgow 'Fair Fortnight' – the summer holiday in the last two weeks in July when traditionally many of the factories and businesses shut up shop. In the days when the road to the Highlands was a single track, it would take us as long as eight hours to drive up north to Mallaig, with my brother and I fighting in the back seat and constantly demanding 'Are we there yet?' while my mother tried to keep us amused with endless games of I-Spy.

My first holiday on my own with friends was in 1977, aged sixteen, on a youth-hostelling trip around Scotland with one of those fantastic cheap railcards that gave you unlimited travel. We started off in Edinburgh, headed to Aberdeen and got as far north as Thurso, as well as exploring all over the west coast and on to Fort William and Ullapool. We had virtually no money, lived off chips and chocolate, and were regularly eaten alive by midges – those nasty wee biting insects that can blight many a trip – but it was a

A 'heilan coo' enjoys the sunshine at Loch Creran, Argyll.
OVERLEAF: A wintery Glen Cova.

fantastic holiday and made me appreciate just how lucky I am to have all this spectacular scenery and fascinating history and culture virtually on my doorstep.

I was also fortunate to be appointed TV-am's Scottish correspondent in 1985 and for the next four years I travelled the length and breadth of the country covering news, current affairs and features for breakfast TV. As well as reporting on disasters like the Piper Alpha oil rig explosion and the Lockerbie terrorist bombing, I was also able to film features and travel pieces. And so I managed to see places that I had always dreamed of visiting. Along with my crew, we travelled to Orkney and the far north of Shetland. We jumped on tiny planes to remote northern islands like Fair Isle and Foula. And on one magical visit to the Outer Hebrides we took the plane that lands on the beach on Barra.

Scotland is where I am happiest. I can be myself and enjoy some of the most exciting and vibrant cities in the world, and also unwind amid spectacular scenic splendour. For me it's all about friends, family, shared experiences and a good sense of humour, and, most important of all, the comfort of being 'home'.

I had always wanted to return to some of those places that mean the most to me and this book is the result. This isn't a definitive guide to Scotland, but it is a journey around the parts of my country that I love very dearly and visit time and time again. I hope you will enjoy my personal Scottish highlights.

The sun sets on the harbour in Pittenweem, one of Scotland's many historic and characterful fishing villages.

DUNDEE

Mains
Castle

Claypotts
Castle

Mills
Observatory

Broughty
Ferry

The
Law

Verdant Works

Tay road
bridge

Broughty
Castle

Tay rail
bridge

Discovery Point
and RRS Discovery

River Tay

N
W   E
S

0   3 miles

DUNDEE
City of Discovery

DUNDEE HAS BEEN MY ADOPTED HOME since 1986, when Steve took me on our first date to show off his city and also to watch his football team in action. We went to see Dundee United vs Hearts at Tannadice, met his pals in the pub afterwards, and I found myself falling in love with both the man and the team, and, of course, the city itself.

We have two football teams here: Dundee United, who play in tangerine and black, and Dundee FC, 'the Dark Blues'. There's obviously a healthy rivalry between the two clubs, but it is generally good-natured and the two sets of supporters are more than likely to buy each other a drink regardless of the final score.

When Steve first took me to see United they were a team with nothing to fear. Managed by the legendary Jim McLean, we could boast about stars like Dave Narey, Paul Hegarty, Maurice Malpas, Paul Sturrock, goalie Hamish McAlpine and my all-time favourite, Eamonn Bannon. My top United moment was during the UEFA cup of 1987 when I saw Kevin Gallacher score at home against the mighty Barcelona just two minutes into the game. That one–nil victory was followed up by a win for United in the second leg at the Nou Camp in Barcelona. I reported on United's progress for TV-am and followed them all the way to the finals in Gothenburg. There has never been, and will never be, a more biased series of match reports transmitted anywhere in the world.

Living in Dundee means that I can now go to most Dundee United home games and I love those Saturday afternoons with a pie at half-time and a drink in the pub afterwards.

If you get yourself to the top of the Law in the heart of Dundee (which, 400 million years ago, was a volcano and later became an Iron Age hill fort), you'll really appreciate how close together the city's two football stadiums are, with Tannadice and Dens Park, home of Dundee FC, diagonally across from each other just yards apart on the same street. You'll also see some spectacular views of the entire city, the River Tay, the road and rail bridges, and across to Fife. On a clear day you can even see all the way to St Andrews.

The original stumps of the old bridge over the River Tay, still clearly visible beside the existing structure.

The Bridge over the Silvery Tay

Look closely at the two-mile-long Dundee rail bridge over the River Tay and you can still see the stumps of the original bridge that crumpled and collapsed on 28 December 1879 during a horrendous storm.

A steam train was actually crossing the bridge when winds reaching gale force 10 caused the high girders in the middle of the bridge to collapse. The engine and six carriages were hurled into the river, killing everyone on board – an estimated seventy-five people.

The disaster was commemorated in a famously bad poem, 'The Tay Bridge Disaster' by the well-meaning William McGonagall, and work on the new bridge began in 1882. It took five years to complete and was opened in 1887 in a very low-key ceremony, in marked contrast to the hoopla of the doomed original.

Steve and I were married in Dundee on 5 September 1992 at Mains Castle. I organized everything locally: flowers, cake, cars, kilt hire, and the hundred and one other details that crop up to stress out the bride-to-be.

The men gave extra-special thrills when they fell over 'dead', revealing themselves as true Scotsmen without a stitch on under their kilts.

It was a brilliant sunny day and a really happy event, and I walked down the aisle to a piper playing 'Bonnie Dundee'. My friends from 'The Clan' – a splendid bunch of Bravehearts who re-enacted ancient Highland battles – provided a guard-of-honour and blood-curdling entertainment. The men gave extra-special thrills when they fell over 'dead', revealing themselves as true Scotsmen without a stitch on under their kilts.

ABOVE: Our wedding day in September 1992 at the beautiful Mains Castle, surrounded by members of 'The Clan'.

OPPOSITE: The magnificent sixteenth-century Mains Castle.

  LORRAINE KELLY'S SCOTLAND

ABOVE: *A bracing boat trip on the River Tay for a close-up view of the bridges.*

OPPOSITE: *Cox's Stack in Lochee is one the few remaining symbols of the old jute trade.*

Dundee has always been known as the city of the three Js: jute, jam and journalism. The jute industry played a major part in the city's prosperity from the mid-nineteenth century until after the Second World War. Raw jute is a vegetable fibre that can be spun into coarse, strong threads and was used to make sailcloth, sacks, carpet backing and tough covering for the wagons that took waves of pioneers across the American Midwest. At its height, there were sixty jute mills employing more than fifty thousand workers in Dundee. Two thirds of those workers were women, many of them Irish immigrants and poorer working-class Dundonians living in the crowded Lochee area of the city. The mills were so noisy that the women learned to lip-read and had their own form of sign language to communicate. Meanwhile, in the late nineteenth century fat cats grew rich on the jute trade with India. The 'jute barons' who owned the mills grew so wealthy that the Dundee suburb of Broughty Ferry, where they built their vast Victorian mansions, once boasted more millionaires per square mile than anywhere else on the planet. The Verdant Works museum, a former jute mill in the Blackness area, gives a real insight into what life was like for the jute workers and how important the trade was to the city.

Cox's Stack, a huge factory chimney in Lochee, is one of the most iconic landmarks of the jute industry. Standing 282 feet (86 metres) tall, it towered over the Camperdown Works, which in 1864 employed over five thousand workers and was the largest factory in the world at that time.

As for the other two Js, legend has it that around 1790, while using up bitter oranges, Janet Keiller from Dundee developed her own marmalade recipe, which her son James began to market successfully. He went on to found a jam and marmalade factory, and Keiller's is still famous all over the world.

Rector of Dundee University

I was lucky enough to be elected rector of Dundee University in 2004. Whenever a new rector is installed they are 'dragged' around the city in a coach pulled by the strongest members of the rugby club, and are obliged to stop off at various hostelries to have a small refreshment. This delightful custom dates back to 1967 when the university became independent (it had previously been part of St Andrews) and was brought in when Sir Peter Ustinov was rector and the Queen Mother was chancellor.

As I was the first female rector in the university's history, the splendid Women's Rugby Club kindly did the honours for me. I didn't get to choose any of my tipples in the various bars we visited, which is why I found myself downing a pint of heavy, followed by a massive glass of absinthe and then some rather odd cocktails. I'm surprised I made it through my inauguration speech.

It was a real honour to be rector for three years and I am very proud of my association with a university that has a worldwide reputation in Life Sciences and carries out groundbreaking work in the School of Medicine at Ninewells Hospital, as well as the creativity that bursts from the renowned Duncan of Jordanstone College of Art and Design.

The university is an important part of Dundee and gives the city centre a real buzz. It has interesting shops, clubs, pubs and restaurants for students and locals alike.

The third J is for journalism. In Dundee that means DC Thomson, founded in 1905 and publishers of the *Dundee Courier* and the *Sunday Post* amongst many others, as well as being responsible for the *Beano*, the *Dandy* and legends like Desperate Dan, Dennis the Menace and the Bash Street Kids.

New industries replaced jute, such as light engineering and electronics. Watching the renaissance of Dundee over the past three decades, after troubled times of industrial unrest and job losses, has been a source of real pride and joy, and the new Victoria and Albert Museum will finally put the city firmly on the map where it belongs. Tourists will come to Dundee to see the V&A in the same way visitors head to Bilbao in the north of Spain to visit the Guggenheim Museum, and then hopefully they will stay to enjoy the most underrated city in Scotland.

Watching the renaissance of Dundee over the past three decades has been a source of real pride and joy.

Dundee has always punched above its weight, but in the past it has been hampered by missing out on the oil boom just an hour up the road in Aberdeen, and by stupid decisions by those in authority who allowed priceless and irreplaceable architecture to be torn down to build monstrous concrete carbuncles. Most of these eyesores – including the monumentally ugly Tayside House – have now rightly been blasted off the face of the earth and, from the rubble, the exciting new waterfront development is slowly emerging.

Right at the heart of the new waterfront, on the River Tay itself, you will find my very favourite museum in all of Scotland. Discovery Point is the setting for RRS *Discovery*, the tough little ship built in Dundee that in 1901 took both Robert Falcon Scott and Ernest Shackleton to Antarctica on the first scientific and geographical exploration of the continent (it was also the last three-masted wooden sailing ship to be built in Britain). Although *Discovery* spent two

OVERLEAF: City Quay at night. Part of the regeneration of Dundee.

years stuck in ice on the coast of Antarctica, the expedition paved the way for the great age of Antarctic exploration that followed. In 1909 Shackleton, who happens to be my all-time hero, almost made it to the South Pole as leader of the Nimrod Expedition. However, he knew that if he didn't turn back he and his men would die and he reckoned his wife Emily would think 'Better a live donkey than a dead lion'. When Scott made his famous attempt on the Pole two years later he was beaten to it by the Norwegian Roald Amundsen and perished on the ice with his men on the way back.

Shackleton himself returned to Antarctica in 1914 to lead an ambitious and ill-fated attempt to trudge across the entire continent. Their ship, the *Endurance*, became trapped in ice 'like a raisin in a wedding cake' and was crushed to smithereens. Shackleton and his men were forced to camp on ice floes for almost five months, before in April 1915 they managed to escape the breaking ice in lifeboats and reached Elephant Island, an uninhabited lump of frozen rock in the middle of the Southern Ocean. In one of the greatest feats of seamanship the world has ever known, Shackleton took five of his companions and sailed eight hundred miles in the worst conditions known to man, heading for a whaling station in South Georgia. After sixteen days' battling fifty-foot waves and bone-freezing cold they reached the island, but they were on the wrong side, miles away from the only human beings and with an unexplored mountain range to cross. The twenty-two men stuck on Elephant Island, however, depended on them getting help, so Shackleton, along with Tom Crean and Frank Worsely, despite being starving, weak and weary, somehow managed to conquer the mountains during a thirty-six-hour climb from hell. Shackleton rescued those left on Elephant Island and didn't lose a single man on that expedition.

He died in 1922 of a heart attack while on yet another expedition to Antarctica and was buried on South Georgia. One day I hope to go there to pay my respects.

Calmer waters for RRS Discovery *after her Antarctic adventures, where she spent two years stuck in ice in the early twentieth century.*

To have the *Discovery* so close to where I live is a constant joy. Not only can you explore every aspect of the ship inside and out, but you can also hire her for special occasions. I had my fiftieth birthday in the wardroom, proudly sitting in Shackleton's chair and enjoying wonderful food and wine. It was quite something to think of Shackleton having also sat at that table with his men, planning their polar adventures.

It was a really enjoyable, atmospheric evening, made even better when Dundee artist Nael Hanna unveiled a wonderful present from Steve – a portrait of our daughter Rosie.

As well as the ship itself, there's an award-winning museum about Antarctica at Discovery Point, and right in front are four statues of emperor penguins with their beaks tucked under their wings as though sheltering from a fierce Antarctic storm. These penguins resulted in my most romantic present ever. Steve knew how much I loved them and managed to track down their sculptor, Tim Chalk, in his studio in Edinburgh and arranged for him to create one for me.

Tim revealed that he had to make the four penguins outside Discovery Point have their heads bowed and tucked under their wings because health and safety officials were worried a distracted passerby might be impaled on their beaks. There was no such problem with my penguin, who stands in our garden with his head up and his beak proudly pointing south.

Dundee is known as the city of *Discovery*, and the little ship that battled all the way to Antarctica is now a symbol not only of all that endures, but also of what we can look forward to in the future. Other attractions include the Dundee Contemporary Arts centre, the McManus Galleries, the Dundee Science Centre and the Dundee Rep. I could go on, but you will just have to come and visit for yourself.

Another reason I love living here is that you come across gems like Claypotts Castle when you are out walking the dog. It has barely altered from when it was first built in the sixteenth century. It is sadly uninhabited, but it has stood quietly watching all the changes to Broughty Ferry and Dundee over the years.

I still commute from Dundee to London every week and feel blessed to have the best of both worlds. I am very proud to be an adopted Dundonian.

OPPOSITE: Shackleton's cabin aboard the RRS Discovery.

BELOW: The imposing medieval Claypotts Castle, one of the five castles in the City of Dundee.

ANGUS,
PERTHSHIRE
and FIFE

Glen Clova

ANGUS

PERTHSHIRE

Glamis Castle

Crannog
Centre

Arbroath

Dunkeld

Bell Rock Lighthouse

Tayport

RAF Leuchars

St Andrews

FIFE

Crail

Anstruther
Pittenweem

Kirkcaldy

North
Queensferry

0   20 miles

N
W   E
S

ANGUS, PERTHSHIRE and FIFE
The delights on my doorstep

LIVING IN DUNDEE, I AM CLOSE enough to be able to enjoy all the glories of Angus, Perthshire and Fife. Here are just some of my favourite places.

Angus

Arbroath, the largest town in Angus, is just up the coast from Dundee and we regularly buy our fresh fish and seafood at the harbour, including the sublime 'Arbroath smokie', one of the great culinary triumphs of Scotland.

The smokie is a haddock smoked over wood; it looks golden on the outside and rich and creamy on the inside. The taste is salty, smoky (as you would expect) and downright delicious.

Everyone has their own way of enjoying a smokie. Some like to eat them right away, especially if they are still hot from the smokehouse, but my favourite method is to grill the smokie with a little butter and then serve it with poached eggs for a fantastic special Sunday breakfast.

Arbroath Football Club has one of the warmest welcomes but one of the coldest grounds in Scotland. Gayfield is right beside the North Sea and whenever I have sat in the wee stand, the wind feels like it will cut you in two; but if you wrap up well and have a pie

The famous Arbroath smokie, a traditional and delicious speciality of smoked fish.

at half-time you will be fine, and it's all part of being a football supporter in Scotland.

A badly timed kick by the goalie or one of the players here can mean the ball is lost for ever, though, for if it leaves the stadium it ends up in the briney. There are tales told of ball boys in days of yore bobbing around in rowing boats, but I think that's just a legend, albeit a good one.

The team, known as the Red Lichties, are in the record books for a splendid 36–nil win over Bon Accord back in 1885, with Jocky Petrie scoring thirteen goals on his own. It's a terrific club, at the

The Declaration of Arbroath

The Declaration of Arbroath is a hugely significant document in Scotland's history. Robert the Bruce defeated England's King Edward II at the Battle of Bannockburn in 1314, but could not be recognized as king because he had earlier been excommunicated by the Pope for murdering a rival to the Scottish throne. Edward II refused to give up claims to rule Scotland, so in 1320, during the continuing wars of independence, a declaration was drawn up at Arbroath Abbey. It was written in Latin, addressed to Pope John XXII and signed by eight Scottish earls and thirty-one barons, asking that Scotland be recognized as an independent nation.

Although the Declaration of Arbroath did not succeed in securing immediate independence – this had to wait for a peace treaty signed by the new English king, Edward III, in 1328 – the document is of immense historical importance. Composed in rousing, passionate language, it is believed to have been the basis for the American Declaration of Independence:

'... as long as a hundred of us remain alive, never will we on any conditions be subject to the lordship of the English. It is in truth not for glory, nor riches, nor honours that we are fighting, but for freedom alone, which no honest man gives up but with life itself.'

heart of the community, and I always enjoy watching games there.

Arbroath is also where you can take a trip to something that should have been impossible to construct. I am stunned by the achievement of those who risked so much to build the Bell Rock Lighthouse – I don't believe it would even be attempted today. Standing 115 feet (35 metres) tall and lying 11 miles east of the Firth of Tay, the lighthouse was built to protect ships from the dreaded Inchcape Reef. Work began in 1807 and finished three long years later. Sixty men with pickaxes were taken to the tiny rock island, which is visible for only four hours a day – the rest of the time it is completely submerged in up to 12 feet (3.5 metres) of water. The men built a wooden shelter on the rock so that they had somewhere to live while they worked, but it must have been freezing, windswept and very, very scary.

The lighthouse was built so well and to such high specifications that, despite the constant crashing of the waves, the stonework at the base hasn't needed to be replaced or altered since it was first laid down two hundred years ago. No wonder this is one of the seven wonders of the industrial world.

You can easily see the Bell Rock from the shore at Arbroath if it is a clear day and you know where to look. The lighthouse became automated in 1998, and the only inhabitants now are sleepy-eyed seals who are so used to tourists that they don't even bother galumphing away, but just stare at you from the rocks during those four hours of low tide.

Just a short boat trip from Arbroath lies Bell Rock, an astonishing feat of engineering and one of the seven wonders of the industrial world.

The beautiful Glamis Castle, birthplace of the late Queen Mother and, legend has it, home to a few ghosts.

Inland from Arbroath, near the town of Forfar, is Glamis Castle, childhood home of our late Queen Mother and considered one of the most beautiful castles in all of Scotland – although as most of our castles have been reduced to rubble, this probably isn't as impressive a claim as it might at first appear.

Legend has it that Glamis was the setting for Shakespeare's *Macbeth* and it is also said to be haunted, but I just enjoy the chance to peek into how the other half lived and see the beautifully kept rooms, as well as having the chance to stroll around the immaculate gardens.

To the north and west, the Angus glens – Clova, Esk, Lethnot, Posen and Glenisla – are glorious, but my favourite is Glen Clova. It's perfect for long walks all year round, although you do have to wrap up carefully in autumn and winter.

It was here that I recently caught sight of a red squirrel – a flash of rich, tawny russet darting up a tree. These timid creatures are becoming shyer and rarer with every passing year, turfed out of their territories by the bigger, more aggressive grey squirrels, but they seem to have found sanctuary in the glens.

Perthshire

When we first came back to Scotland when Rosie was eleven and ready to start 'big school', we lived near Blairgowrie in glorious Perthshire. It's such a beautiful part of the country, with stunning scenery such as the famous Queen's View overlooking Loch Tummel and thought by some to have been named after Queen Victoria, who dearly loved Scotland (and one crusty Highlander in particular, if we are to believe the movie *Mrs Brown*, starring Dame Judi Dench and Billy Connolly).

Victoria was also an admirer of the Hermitage, near Dunkeld – a sort of modest forerunner of present-day amusement parks. The Hermitage Pleasure Ground was created in the mid to late eighteenth century in the grounds of Dunkeld House by the rather eccentric Duke of Atholl. He wanted guests to have an unforgettable

The famous Queen's View overlooking Loch Tummel is thought by some to have been named after Queen Victoria, who dearly loved Scotland.

experience as they visited his house and grounds, which include a splendid waterfall. He built a stone viewing pavilion, known as Ossian's Hall, which projected over the edge of the gorge to give the best possible views of the falls, and Queen Victoria was apparently enchanted by the circular mirrored room.

The little town of Dunkeld nearby is one of my favourite places in Perthshire. Even though it's another ruin, the cathedral is mightily impressive. Dunkeld also has gorgeous little shops and eating places, and it is one of the training centres for local army cadets.

I am very honoured to be Honorary Colonel of the Black Watch Cadets, and have really enjoyed meeting the adult volunteers and the young people who gain so much from the organization. Not all of them go on to join the armed forces, but whatever they do in life they will be all the better for their time in the cadets, where they make friends, learn to work as a team and to look out for one another.

A really quirky and fascinating look into the past can be found at the Scottish Crannog Centre on Loch Tay, near Aberfeldy, where I used to go years ago on school trips. The powers-that-be thought us Glaswegian children should get some fresh air into our lungs and enjoy hill walking, canoeing and sightseeing. We really loved these trips.

The Crannog Centre is a painstakingly faithful recreation of a type of ancient dwelling built right in the water, possibly for defence purposes, but maybe just a way of showing off how rich and powerful a family or clan might have been 2,500 years ago.

The famous and glorious Queen's View overlooking Loch Tummel.

OVERLEAF: The atmospheric and eerie Hermitage near Dunkeld, with Ossian's Hall, a viewing pavilion that extends right over the gorge.

Kinnoull Hill is easy to reach on foot from Perth and at the top there are truly stunning views of not only the River Tay and Perthshire but, on a clear day, all the way north to the Highlands. Kinnoull Tower was built as a folly in 1829 by Lord Grey of Kinfauns and was supposed to be a copy of those fairy-tale German castles along the banks of the Rhine, which were hugely popular in the nineteenth century.

The Kingdom of Fife

Fifers have somehow managed to hold on to their title of 'kingdom' despite some oppressively dull name changes inflicted on the rest of Scotland by officials. It's a relatively small area but contains upmarket St Andrews, RAF Leuchars air base, the big towns of Kirkcaldy and Dunfermline, and picturesque fishing villages.

We had a little holiday home in Tayport during the time we lived down south, and we spent lots of breaks and weekends there. Our place was right by the river and we enjoyed beachcombing and seeing seals and dolphins frolicking in the water.

We were also just fifteen minutes from St Andrews, famous as the home of golf and also more

River Tay from Kinnoull Hill, on a glorious autumn's day.

Taking to the skies

I really wanted to be a fighter pilot when I was growing up, but back in the 1970s there were no female flyers in the RAF. Times have changed and, quite rightly, the first female pilot joined the Red Arrows in 2011.

I did, however, manage to fulfil my ambition of flying in a jet when I was taken up in a Tornado to help launch the famous air show at RAF Leuchars in 2006. My pilot was the suitably dashing Pete 'Brommers' Brombley, who gave me the safety talk, helped me into my 'G suit' and handed me a clutch of sick bags, which I am happy and proud to say I didn't need.

We flew at 700 miles an hour, upside down at times, and pulled four and a half Gs (that's four and a half times the force of gravity). Flying at that speed means blood drains from your head and you would pass out if you weren't wearing the special suit that forces it all back up again. I described it as like being cuddled by a gorilla. It was a thrilling, unforgettable experience and a real insight into just how skilled our pilots need to be.

recently where Prince William met and fell in love with Kate Middleton. St Andrews is a classy town with a rich history and a venerable university, founded in 1413, one of the oldest education establishments in the world. They've been playing golf here for over six hundred years and, if you love the game, the Old Course is likely to be at the top of your wish list. A sliced tee shot from the first would land firmly on the famous beach where the movie *Chariots of Fire* was filmed. The beach is the perfect spot for a bracing walk, and I also love to potter around the specialist shops in town and have a coffee and a catch-up with friends.

Heading out of St Andrews, the East Neuk of Fife has a wealth of beaches, fishing villages like Anstruther and Crail, and old-fashioned charm. I often head here for a day trip – not just for the best fish suppers money can buy, but also for a walk along the harbours to look at the boats and marvel at the bravery and tenacity of our fishermen.

Pittenweem in particular has admirably held on to its sense of history and real character. The paving stones near the harbour wall were once carefully numbered for the fishing boats to land their catches. First back to harbour would tie up at the number one spot, second at number two, and so on. This was hugely important, as the fish was sold in strict order of which boat had arrived back first. After the practice was discontinued the pier was resurfaced. No longer needed, the numbers were put back higgledy-piggeldy.

At North Queensferry in Fife there's a cracking view of the Forth rail bridge, a true Scottish icon. 'Painting the Forth Bridge' is a phrase that has been used since the bridge was completed in 1890. We might need to think of another description for a never-ending job of work, though, because advances in technology mean that the most recent facelift and brand-new coat of shiny red paint applied in 2011 will last for a good twenty years or more.

I'm incredibly lucky to have all this so close by and to be able to enjoy day trips to such an interesting and fascinating part of Scotland.

The jumbled number stones at Pittenweem Harbour, originally used by fishermen to order the catch of the day.

OVERLEAF: Sunrise at Crail Harbour in the picturesque East Neuk of Fife.

EDINBURGH

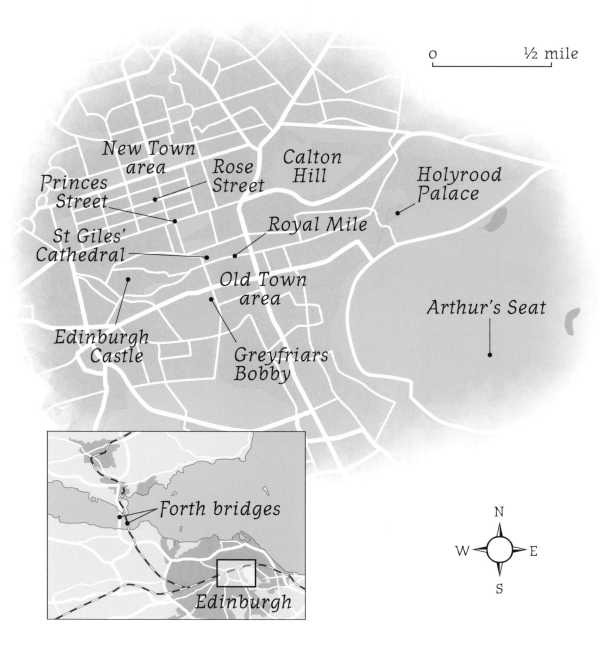

New Town area

Rose Street

Calton Hill

Holyrood Palace

Princes Street

Royal Mile

St Giles' Cathedral

Old Town area

Arthur's Seat

Edinburgh Castle

Greyfriars Bobby

0   ½ mile

Forth bridges

Edinburgh

N
W   E
S

EDINBURGH
Scotland's elegant yet earthy capital

I REMEMBER ARRIVING IN EDINBURGH BACK IN the summer of 1980, pushing a pram while wearing roller skates. I was taking part in a foolhardy fundraiser for the British Heart Foundation that saw me roller-skating fifty miles from the 'heart' of East Kilbride to the Heart of Midlothian, a heart-shaped mosaic on the pavement of the Royal Mile, just outside St Giles' Cathedral. It is apparently considered good luck to spit on the mosaic, but I just thought it would be the perfect spot to end my charity rollerthon.

There was just one tiny problem. I couldn't actually roller-skate all that well, and I didn't make much progress in the run-up to the big day, which is why I decided to borrow a large old-fashioned pram to cling on to – a sort of Zimmer frame with wheels. It took me from first light until late at night to cover the first forty miles and I limped the last ten the following morning.

I already knew Edinburgh well by that time because I'd attended college there the year before as part of my training as a cub reporter on the *East Kilbride News*. I was sent to Napier College for three months, along with other young journalists from all over Scotland, to learn about law, shorthand, local government and how to put a story together. It was the best of both worlds for me. I had the security of a job as well as the life of a student and the chance to explore Scotland's capital city.

Of course, a lot of my time was taken up doing vital research on the infamous 'Rose Street crawl' – a wonderful custom that involves visiting as many pubs as possible on the long and lively road that runs parallel to Princes Street.

Although Edinburgh's most famous shopping street has recently been blighted by the madness of installing the grotesquely expensive tram system, Princes Street has managed to survive the years of closure and building work. It might be a bit tattier than before, but no other high street in the world can boast such a splendid view as that of the famous Edinburgh Castle.

There's a fine Edinburgh tradition where a gun is fired from the castle ramparts at precisely 1 p.m. every day. It scares the bejesus out of tourists, but Edinburgh citizens don't turn a hair, although some might casually check their watches just to be sure they are keeping proper time. Believe it or not, though, there's not a day goes by that some daft visitor doesn't pose the question, 'What time does the one o'clock gun go off?' to staff at the castle.

Looking up to the imposing fortress of Edinburgh Castle in the heart of Edinburgh's Old Town.

Greyfriars Bobby

There's a charming little statue of a cute Skye terrier at the corner of Candlemaker Row and the George IV Bridge in the heart of Edinburgh. It stands close to Greyfriars Kirk, where the little dog loyally kept vigil by the graveside of his master, night watchman John Gray, for fourteen long years until his little heart gave out on 14 January 1872.

Bobby is one of the most famous dogs in the world and Walt Disney even made a movie of his story. In recent years the tale has been debunked, with sceptics claiming it was little more than a Victorian myth to attract tourists to Edinburgh and drum up custom for local businesses. They claim that although Bobby did live in the kirkyard, he was a very happy wee dog and didn't lie whining pitifully on the grave of his master, but enjoyed being spoiled and chasing rats.

On the premise that you should never let the truth get in the way of a good story, I much prefer to believe that Bobby was a loyal friend, ever true, mourning his master for all those years.

I had rather an unfortunate encounter of my own with the one o'clock gun. As an Honorary Colonel of the Black Watch Cadets, I was asked to launch Armed Forces Day in Edinburgh in 2011. It involved taking a ride in a helicopter and being winched down to Calton Hill, just east of Princes Street, before firing a gun at exactly the same time as the famous one across in the castle: 1 p.m. precisely.

All went according to plan: I was picked up at RAF Leuchars in Fife and enjoyed the helicopter ride to Edinburgh, especially the bit where we were low-flying along Princes Street and waving to startled shoppers. I was winched down with expertise by the RAF – and then things unravelled somewhat.

I was told that as soon as I heard the sergeant major shout 'Fire!' I had to press the button and fire the cannon. Simple. In my state of giddy nervousness, though, when I heard the countdown begin at 'five' I thought he had barked 'Fire!' and I set off the gun a full five seconds early.

I was told that as soon as I heard the sergeant major shout 'Fire!' I had to press the button and fire the cannon. Simple.

The assembled ranks of army, navy and air force were clutching themselves and hooting with laughter, and my feeble attempt to blame it on the one o'clock gun going off late didn't work for a nanosecond. It just proves that you should never get a civvy to do a job meant for a man (or woman) in uniform.

I am really drawn to the Old Town of Edinburgh with its cobbled streets, old closes, steep stone steps and atmospheric medieval and Gothic architecture. The area around the Grassmarket, in particular, is buzzing with interesting, quirky shops and pubs, clubs and restaurants. There might be a lot of tourist tat on the Royal Mile, the steep hill that joins the castle with Holyrood Palace, but you still have gems like The Witchery restaurant, City Chambers and the splendid St Giles' Cathedral, where I finished my roller-skate all those years ago.

Night-time view of Edinburgh Castle and the Church of St Cuthbert's.

ABOVE: *Arthur's Seat overlooking Waverley Station.*

OPPOSITE: *Enjoying a stunning view of Edinburgh in the sunshine, with Arthur's Seat in the background.*

At the very bottom of the Royal Mile, Holyrood Palace looks rather disapprovingly over at the new Scottish Parliament building. I would like to say that this odd-looking structure has grown on me, but I reckon it's become even uglier since it was opened for business back in 2004, almost £400 million over budget. The interior is impressive, though, and so are the views of Arthur's Seat enjoyed by the politicians and civil servants.

Few cities can boast such an impressive hill right at their centre. Arthur's Seat, the remnants of a volcano, towers 250 metres (822 feet) above Holyrood Park and the views out over Edinburgh and the Firth of Forth from its summit are unforgettable.

57

The Georgian New Town is in stark contrast to the crowded, crooked medieval Old Town and is sumptuously well planned and dignified, with broad, open streets and neoclassical buildings. These two polar opposite parts of the same city give Edinburgh a unique character. It always makes me think of a seemingly rather uptight woman who likes to kick her heels up after a few drinks and enjoy a good time.

Edinburgh is also rightly renowned for the two-week-long Festival and Fringe in August every year, and although sometimes the Fringe performers outnumber the audience, it's a big bubble

Looking through Edinburgh's majestic New Town and across the Firth of Forth to Fife.

Spot the difference. I always wanted to be a cartoon.

OVERLEAF: The steep climb up Arthur's Seat is well worth the view.

of excitement and creativity, and once again debunks the myth of Edinburgh being rather stuffy.

Aside from the Festival, the city has a ridiculous number of art galleries and museums where locals and visitors can happily wallow. If you have even an iota of interest in the arts, you really must visit both the National Gallery of Scotland and the Scottish National Gallery of Modern Art, and give yourself plenty of time.

My personal favourite is the Scottish National Portrait Gallery in Queen Street, and I was chuffed to be immortalized there as one of the subjects of the exhibition of Fizzers caricatures in 2007 by the Scottish Cartoon Art Studio. It was the first time I'd shared a room with Billy Connolly, Ewan McGregor, Sir Sean Connery, Sir Alex Ferguson, Brian Cox and Annie Lennox at the same time, even if it was just their 'Fizzers', or faces, hanging on the wall.

Some of my happiest memories are all wrapped in Edinburgh. I have presented the live New Year TV show from a balcony on Princes Street, looking down over one of the biggest parties in the world. It's always a frenetic but fun programme, but oh so stressful as you *must* hit the bells dead on time at midnight.

I always feel part of something truly Scottish celebrating New Year live on air, especially as you know that all over the world, from Alaska to Zanzibar, people are singing our song, 'Auld Lang Syne' by the genius Ayrshire bard Robert Burns.

I've also spent hours trudging the streets of Edinburgh, and not just when I was a student trying in vain to get a taxi after a night out. I've taken part in eight twenty-six-mile midnight Moonwalks in aid of breast cancer charities, but one of the best was in Edinburgh in 2010 with my mum and my daughter Rosie. Walking up the Royal Mile with thousands of other women all dressed in bright, multi-coloured decorated bras was something I will always remember; and so will all of those blokes, pouring out of the pubs, entranced at the sight of so many bouncing bosoms. It's a tough walk, right up Arthur's Seat, past Leith and into Portobello, but

the views of the famous Forth bridges as the sun is coming up make the tiredness and blisters well worth it.

It was also in Edinburgh that I was awarded an OBE from the Queen at Holyrood Palace in 2012, the year of her Diamond Jubilee. The honour was completely unexpected and it was a day to treasure.

I did a live broadcast for my breakfast TV show from the gates of the palace, and then along with Steve and Rosie,

and my mum and dad, I was ushered into the palace. You are taken into a plush room with all the other people being honoured, and an impossibly plummy but kindly man in livery takes you through the protocol. I have never been more nervous in my life, but I did feel better when a white-faced RAF hero, wearing a uniform festooned in medals for bravery, said he would rather be facing the Taliban than going through such an ordeal.

I actually cried through the whole ceremony, and to this day I have absolutely no idea what the Queen said to me. Her Majesty is obviously used to dealing with overwhelmed subjects because she smiled very kindly as she gently eased me away with a firm handshake and congratulations.

It was a lovely day, made even more special by meeting others being honoured and hearing their stories of courage, service and hard work. Edinburgh has truly given me some unforgettable golden moments.

LEFT: The iconic Forth rail bridge.

ABOVE: Honoured by the Queen at Holyrood Palace in 2012, the year of her Diamond Jubilee.

GLASGOW

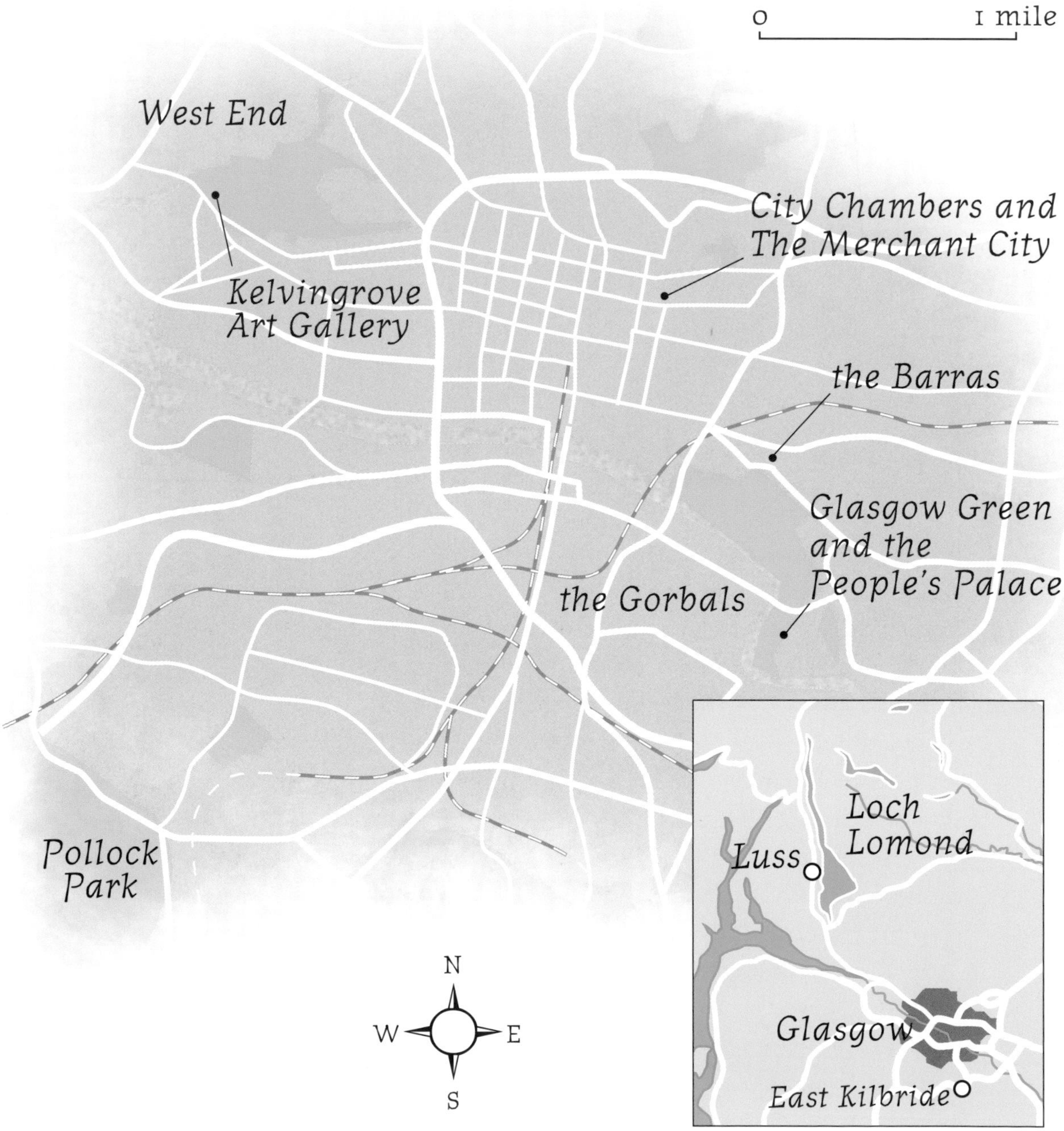

West End

Kelvingrove
Art Gallery

City Chambers and
The Merchant City

the Barras

Glasgow Green
and the
People's Palace

the Gorbals

Pollock
Park

0   1 mile

N
W   E
S

Loch
Lomond

Luss

Glasgow

East Kilbride

GLASGOW
The 'dear green place' and city of my birth

I WAS BORN IN GLASGOW AND I am sure that is one of the main reasons I ended up being a journalist. Glaswegians are renowned for being friendly and welcoming, but they are also very inquisitive and more than a wee bit cheeky. If you are waiting in the queue for a bus it won't be long before a wee woman who is 'aff her heid with her feet' will be telling you her life story and expecting you to follow suit. Take a taxi in Glasgow and be prepared to be quizzed on everything from football to politics. It's one of the many things I love about this ballsy, brash but big-hearted city.

My mum and dad were just teenagers when they married in 1959 and I arrived shortly afterwards, on 30 November that year. At the age of eighteen, with very little money, my young parents set up home together in the Gorbals, once the most deprived and notorious slum in Europe. That was back when Glasgow gained its 'no mean city' reputation, but when I was a baby the slum clearances were in full swing.

We soon upgraded from that 'single end' – living in just one room that served as a kitchen/living room, with a bed in a recess in the wall, and with no hot water and an outside toilet – to a vastly improved room and kitchen in Bridgeton in the east end of the city. It meant that my mum and dad and me and my baby brother Graham still shared a bedroom, but we did have the luxury of an inside loo.

ABOVE LEFT: As a toddler in the Gorbals.

ABOVE RIGHT: Aged eleven outside our tenement in Bridgeton.

OPPOSITE: My wee granny Margaret Kelly, shortly before she died in 2013.

My dad, who was a TV engineer, worked incredibly hard and put in colossal amounts of overtime to give us a good start in life. My parents also taught me how to read and write before I started Strathclyde Primary School. The school was right on the banks of the River Clyde and, although it was frowned upon, once the school bell rang at 4 p.m. and set us free we would head for the paths along the river and play cowboys and Indians, Bonnie and Clyde, and even re-enact school productions like *West Side Story* with the Sharks versus the Jets. There were always scraps and fights, but our teachers were dedicated and inspirational. They took no nonsense, even from the wildest kids.

I went back to revisit all my old childhood haunts as part of a feature for GMTV on how to trace your ancestors. The single end in Ballater Street in the Gorbals was long gone, replaced by shiny new flats as part of the regeneration of the area. The tenement in Swanston Street in Bridgeton had been razed to the ground in the seventies and it was hard to get my bearings, as even the layout of the streets had changed.

It was fascinating to learn about my past during the making of that programme. Glasgow's famous Mitchell Library was a brilliant source of material and helped us discover that the Kellys were originally from Draperston in Northern Ireland. Like so many Irish people, in the late nineteenth century, they had fled to Glasgow in search of work. The men grafted in the shipyards and the family eventually ended up in the Gorbals. It was a hard life, but my grandmother Margaret always talked about the community spirit, especially amongst the women, who all helped each other to cope with illness, poverty and men who drank too much. Life was tough, particularly between the wars, and it was these tenacious women who worked their fingers to the bone to keep families together.

I used to love getting the bus into Glasgow city centre to look at the shops, and also spent many happy weekends at the Barras, a bustling market and home of the famous Barrowland Ballroom, voted the best music venue in the UK in 2005 by the people who know best – the British bands who actually perform all over the country. In the market I really used to enjoy the cabaret of the salesmen with their non-stop patter, flogging everything from teapots to curtains. A bag of boiled whelks cost pennies and lasted for ages, because you had to dig them out of their shells with a pin after slathering them in vinegar.

When I was thirteen, a man with a clipboard came and told us our tenement was being demolished and we were being moved to the new town of East Kilbride, just to the south-east of the city. This was where I went to secondary school, and got my first big break by landing a job as a cub reporter on the *East Kilbride News*, but I really missed living in Glasgow.

One night when I was heading back to East Kilbride on the bus from a night out in Glasgow's West End, I noticed that there were some flats being built right across from the station. This was 1983 and the start of people moving back to the heart of the city centre. You could feel real change in the air. I wanted to stand on my own two feet and move back to Glasgow, and this was the perfect opportunity. I decided to take a look at one of the flats.

I got my first big break by landing a job as a cub reporter on the **East Kilbride News**, *but I really missed living in Glasgow.*

It was tiny, with one bedroom and a living room where you couldn't swing a kitten. I had just landed a job with BBC Scotland in the leafy West End of Glasgow, with a resulting substantial loss in wages, so it was tough to scrape together the money to pay the mortgage. I ended up taking on a job as a waitress at the then achingly trendy Charlie Parker's Diner. My stint at the BBC led to a job as a reporter with TV-am in 1985. The small studio in George Square happened to be a three-minute walk away from my flat, right at the bottom of the hill where I lived, so it was the perfect base from which to cover the whole of Scotland.

It was only once I'd moved back into the city that I really got to know it properly. At that time the city centre was going through a real overhaul, which culminated in Glasgow beating off competition from Paris, Athens and Amsterdam to be declared European City of Culture in 1990. I watched as it was transformed – first of all in a very practical way, when the black grime was blasted from the overblown Victorian civic buildings, like the

Glasgow City Chambers, a prime example of Victorian architecture.
OVERLEAF: The changing Glasgow skyline reflected in the River Clyde.

City Chambers in George Square, and also from the tenements in the West End, to reveal a golden city. New restaurants, pubs and clubs sprang up to complement older, established institutions and, although Glaswegians have always been fiercely proud of their city, now there was a new swagger.

Within walking distance from George Square is a district of Glasgow known as the Merchant City, famous for its restored Victorian warehouses, upmarket eating places and shops. In the West End, the bars and restaurants on the cobbled streets of Ashton Lane have always been a favourite of mine, and there's always music, from buskers, established performers and up-and-coming young bands.

There's a real buzz about the city centre and, just like when I was a kid, I love to walk around window-shopping, people-watching and soaking up the atmosphere. You can saunter down Sauchiehall Street and pop into the Willow Tea Rooms, designed in 1904 by the world-renowned Charles Rennie Mackintosh, whose distinctive art nouveau designs can be found on everything from tea towels to fridge magnets.

Glasgow means 'dear green place' in Gaelic, and while that might seem a bit of a misnomer for such a busy, bustling city with a motorway running right through its very heart, it's actually extremely apt, as there are so many beautiful parks and open spaces. One of the joys for me growing up was all of that beautiful countryside right on our doorstep.

As a kid I loved Glasgow Green and visiting the People's Palace, a truly wonderful museum that tells the story of the city with the focus on how ordinary people led their lives, from earliest times to the present day. Especially interesting is the Victorian era, when Glasgow was the second city of the British Empire. As is always the case, a select few made massive fortunes off the back of the working classes, many of whom, like my ancestors, had come over from Ireland looking for work.

The Finnieston crane, a reminder of the proud history of shipbuilding on the Clyde.

The People's Palace in Glasgow Green, opened in 1898 to provide a cultural centre for residents, tells the story of the city.

Glasgow has an impressive twenty museums and art galleries (the vast majority are free to enter), with both the Kelvingrove Art Gallery and the Burrell Collection being real stand-outs.

A legend persists that the Kelvingrove Gallery was built back to front – that is, with its back to the road – because of a mistake by the architect, who then killed himself by jumping from one of the towers. This is an urban myth that just won't go away, but there's no truth in it; the main entrance was always intended to be in Kelvingrove Park. A few years ago the museum underwent a massive transformation and was re-opened in 2006. As well as works by Rembrandt, Van Gogh and Leonardo da Vinci, you can also see the astonishing Salvador Dali painting *Christ of Saint John of the Cross*.

The Burrell Collection in Glasgow's Pollock Park is one of the largest, most eclectic and exciting collections ever amassed by one individual, the shipping magnate Sir William Burrell. In 1944 he donated all eight thousand objects, ranging from paintings by Degas,

The imposing entrance of the 'back-to-front' Kelvingrove Gallery, one of Glasgow's many impressive museums and galleries.

sculptures by Rodin, medieval stained glass and ancient artefacts from Egypt and China. Again, admission is free and Pollock Park is another of those green spaces for which the city is famous.

When I was a small child just about everyone in Glasgow took their holidays during the 'Fair Fortnight' in July. The schools shut, the factories closed and, before cheap package deals to Spain were ever thought of, you went 'doon the watter' to the west coast seaside towns of Ayr, Saltcoats, Seamill and Troon, or up to the Trossachs and Loch Lomond.

Loch Lomond

You take the high road and I'll take the low road . . . but it doesn't really matter how you get there, as long as you eventually end up by the shores of this big, beautiful loch. It might not have the cachet of being home to a monster, but Loch Lomond is one of my favourite places, and it's a really easy day trip from Glasgow.

The bonnie, bonnie banks

I remember belting out 'The Bonnie Banks o' Loch Lomond' along with fifty thousand other fans at an outdoor Run Rig concert on the banks of the loch itself back in 1991. The fantastic Gaelic rock band's version was voted Scotland's greatest song in 2008, but there has always been some debate as to the meaning of the lyrics.

Some believe the song is about two Highlanders captured during the Jacobite Uprising in the early eighteenth century. One of them was released and was able to take the 'high road' back home, but the other was put to death and on the 'low road', so that only his spirit could return to Scotland and to Loch Lomond. Alternatively, it is also interpreted as a pure and simple love song.

It's the largest loch in Scotland and the biggest expanse of fresh water in Britain. The scenic splendour is dominated by Ben Lomond, one of the most popular Munros (hills in Scotland over 3,000 feet/914 metres) because it is so accessible. Both the loch and the ben are part of the Loch Lomond and The Trossachs National Park, Scotland's first national park.

The little village of Luss, right by the west shore of the loch, will for ever have a place in my affection as the setting for Scottish soap *Take the High Road*, which ran from 1980 until 2003, and although it's a bit touristy, nothing can take away from the sheer charm of the neat cottages and the beautiful setting.

As well as boat trips from busy Balloch to the islands scattered on the loch, you can also land by seaplane, and there are plenty of safe places for a picnic and a chilly swim. There are also good cycle paths along the shore and it's a brilliant place for serious walking; part of the famous West Highland Way runs along the east shore of the loch, with hardy hikers making their way from Milngavie to Fort William.

Next stop: the Highlands.

With my gorgeous border terrier Rocky on the banks of Loch Lomond.

HIGHLANDS

Ben Nevis

Ben Nevis is a towering presence, looming over Fort William and proudly standing 4,406 feet (1,343 metres) above sea level, the highest peak in Britain. You can reach the summit if you are reasonably fit and it is firmly at the top of my 'to do' list. Right now I am just happy to admire the view.

Ben Nevis, Scotland's highest mountain, towering over Fort William and reflected in Loch Linnhe.

Walk on the wild side

There have been many weird and wonderful ascents of Ben Nevis – most of them quirky ways to raise money for charity.

We've had students pushing a bed up to the top, a brave man carrying a barrel of beer and even a piano was humped up to the summit. But perhaps bravest of all was the blonde fundraiser who strode to the peak in nothing but hiking boots and an itsy-bitsy, teeny-weeny bikini.

Glenfinnan

At the top of Loch Shiel in Lochaber stands the Glenfinnan Monument, built on the spot where Bonnie Prince Charlie raised his standard and rallied his troops for the start of the doomed Jacobite Uprising of 1745. It was here that he waited as the clans gathered, before claiming the Scottish and English thrones on behalf of his father James, 'the Old Pretender', son of the deposed King James II.

This monument – an unknown Highlander on top of a tower – is a tribute to all of those who died fighting for the prince, and I have always admired its quiet dignity.

Just a short walk away is the Glenfinnan Viaduct made famous by the Harry Potter movies as part of the train journey that took Harry and his gang to Hogwarts. It's a remarkable example of Victorian engineering, built as part of the West Highland Railway between Mallaig and Fort William. For the full Harry Potter experience you can take a trip across the viaduct on the Jacobite Steam Train in the summer.

OPPOSITE: The Glenfinnan Viaduct had a starring role in the Harry Potter films.

ABOVE: The Glenfinnan Monument, where Bonnie Prince Charlie raised his standard in 1745 and waited for the clans to gather.

Mountains of Myth

Not only glorious to behold, and easily seen from the main road, the stunning mountain range to the north of Glen Shiel is also the subject of many a legend, including this one, my favourite, about the five sisters of Kintail:

Originally there were seven sisters, all very beautiful and living near Loch Duich. Two young men sailed into the loch one day and fell in love with the two youngest sisters. They wanted to marry, but the sisters' father said the elder sisters would have to be betrothed first.

The young men said they had five older brothers and promised they would bring them back to Loch Duich to marry the five older sisters. Well, the two happy couples left and never came back. The five sisters waited and waited, but eventually turned into stone. They are still waiting in Kintail for their husbands, who will never arrive.

The South Glen Shiel Munros. Sheer Highland splendour.

Is that a monster behind us? I'm scarier than Nessie.

Loch Ness

We had a chilly but really fun holiday on Loch Ness when my daughter Rosie was three. We hired a boat for a week and tootled up and down the loch looking for Nessie, the famous monster. Every ripple and shadow might just be that elusive beastie, and although you know in your head that it must be nonsense, it doesn't stop you scouring the waters because you hope in your heart that it's true. You might just be the lucky one who snatches a quick photo of Nessie. I'm constantly amazed that she tends to make an appearance just at the start of the tourist season. Funny, that.

The little town of Drumnadrochit on the shore of the loch is the centre for monster lovers. There's a whole Nessie industry, with cheap and cheerful tat, lurid green soft toys, key rings, fridge magnets and tea towels, and even Nessie ice-cream cones and burgers. For those disappointed not to have seen her, there's a giant plastic replica that kids clamber over to get their photo taken.

Away from the tourist traps, Loch Ness has some scenic gems, including the picture-perfect Urquhart Castle – sadly another ruin, but a strangely noble and elegant one.

Culloden

Near Inverness lies Culloden, where in 1746 the last ever full-scale battle on British soil was fought. It was the end of Bonnie Prince Charlie's ambitions, and resulted in the bloody slaughter of his brave Highlanders.

Charlie had come to Scotland from France to oust the German Hanoverians from the throne and restore the Stuart dynasty. He gathered an army of loyal clansmen from the Highlands, and these Jacobites marched to Edinburgh, defeating King George II's forces at the Battle of Prestonpans. They pushed on towards London and managed to march as far south as Derby, before turning back when it became clear that hoped-for support from the French and English would never materialize.

Culloden was the last stand.

The poignant and deeply atmospheric Culloden battlefield, where many brave Highlanders lost their lives.

At Drummossie Moor the exhausted, outnumbered and ill-equipped Highlanders faced the Duke of Cumberland and his government troops. The Jacobites were mown down by Cumberland's artillery as they waited to charge. It was disorganized and hopeless. The Jacobites were defeated, hunted down like animals and slaughtered. Two thousand Highlanders and around five hundred English government troops died. Cumberland was reviled as 'a butcher' and Bonnie Prince Charlie hightailed it back to France.

Today Culloden is a bleak but highly emotional and evocative war memorial. Every time I visit I get goosebumps. The moor has been restored to how it would have looked in 1746, with flags marking the positions of the clans and Cumberland's troops. The small stones scattered there, each etched with the name of one of the decimated clans, are heartbreaking in their simplicity.

Today Culloden is a bleak but highly emotional and evocative war memorial. Every time I visit I get goosebumps.

In the aftermath of Culloden, the wearing of the kilt was banned, as was the playing of bagpipes; even speaking Gaelic. The victors wanted to guarantee that there would never again be an uprising to threaten the crown, and they were merciless. This crushing of the clans was also a factor in one of the most shameful episodes in Scottish history – the Highland Clearances. From the late eighteenth to the mid-nineteenth century rich landlords, often with government support, turned vast areas of their land over to profitable sheep farming. This meant that across Scotland, and particularly in the Highlands, many people were forcibly evicted from their homes and the land their families had farmed, often for generations. Thousands of men, women and children watched as their houses were burnt to the ground and their way of life destroyed. The Clearances marked the end of traditional clan society and culture. Many set sail to America, Canada, Australia and New Zealand, and though the hard-working Scottish diaspora made its mark in the New World, it's sad to think of the strength, intelligence and ingenuity that was lost to Scotland.

John o' Groats

John o' Groats, which is wrongly believed by many people to be the most northerly place in Britain, used to be pretty grotty and a real let-down for those intrepid souls who had walked, cycled, jogged or hopped all the way up from Land's End to raise money for charity. There have been big improvements over the past couple of years, though, and it is no longer a source of embarrassment. It's named after Jan de Groot, who got a licence for the first ferry between there and South Ronaldsay in the Orkney Islands in the 1490s.

The actual most northerly point of the Scottish mainland is a bit further up at Dunnet Head, but it's John o' Groats that clings to the title. For a fee you can even have your name emblazoned on the famous signpost for a souvenir photograph, and of course I had to do it.

This photo is a must, even though technically John o' Groats isn't the most northerly part of the Scottish mainland.

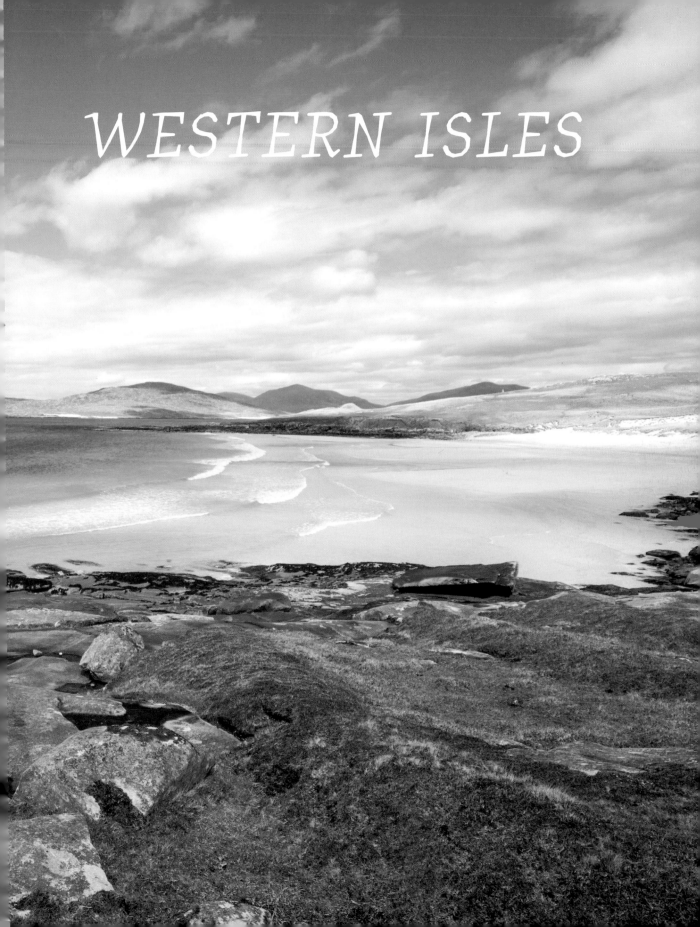

WESTERN ISLES

Back in the eighties I came to film the magical process that turns water, barley, yeast and peat into Islay single malt for a special feature for TV-am's Sunday programme, presented by David Frost. While the crew set up some shots in the storeroom where the whisky matures in giant barrels, I was given a fascinating tour of the whole process. When I came back to see the crew, their eyes were rolling around their heads: they'd been given a cheeky nip of whisky in its virtually raw state, and it's a bit like drinking rocket fuel.

After that first trip I'd always wanted to revisit Islay, and also to go across to neighbouring Jura, which somehow seemed remote and just out of reach, even though it's merely a quick sail on the ferry from Islay. This time we stayed in Islay's main town, Bowmore, dominated by a picture-postcard distillery and a splendid round white church at the top of the hill. Apparently it was built in the shape of a circle so that there were no corners for the devil to hide in.

While we were there we had a special tour of Bowmore, Islay's first distillery, right by the shores of Loch Indaal, where they have been making whisky since 1779. Just as on my first trip in 1985, our guide was the redoubtable Eddie MacAffer, now distillery manager and a man who knows all there is to know about creating the perfect dram.

Barley is one of the key ingredients of whisky and before it can be used it has to be malted. To start the process of germination, the barley is soaked and spread over a stone malting floor. At Bowmore they then turn the barley over by hand, using special tools. It has to be turned every four hours, day and night, for up to a week. Eddie made it look effortless, but when I tried to give it a go I was exhausted after a couple of minutes and couldn't get into the proper rhythm. It's back-breaking, dedicated work. At the end of this process you are left with 'green malt', which then has to be dried to stop the germination process temporarily. It's put into a massive kiln, and it is the heat and smoke from the peat fire at the bottom that add that distinctive Islay smoky taste and smell.

The dried malt is ground down to grist and then goes into the mash house, where the grist is mixed with three lots of water, each at a higher

temperature, so that the starch in the grain is converted into liquid sugar or 'wort'; it is now well on its way to being turned into alcohol.

Now it starts to get really interesting. The liquid wort is pumped into 'wash backs' – massive vessels holding thousands of litres. Yeast is added and so begins fermentation. It looks as though the mixture is being churned up by a giant super-whisk, but the bubbling and churning is simply caused by the yeast feeding on the sugar and naturally converting the mixture into alcohol. The malty, beery smell is overwhelming and really heady, but not in a bad way.

At Bowmore their No. 1 vaults are the oldest on the island and the only ones below sea level. It's cold, damp and dark down there.

Now the liquid wash is distilled in the still house by being boiled. The resulting hot vapours are captured and cooled and the condensed liquid alcohol is collected and run through a padlocked spirit safe. This allows the makers to check on the spirit but keeps the Excise man happy because no alcohol can be siphoned off illegally. The liquid is then put into oak sherry casks, some going all the way back to 1957, before I was even born. All it needs now is to be given time to grow up and mature in the vaults.

At Bowmore their No. 1 vaults are the oldest on the island and the only ones below sea level. It's cold, damp and dark down there – perfect conditions for whisky to come of age. Down in the vaults, as the whisky in the casks matures, around 2 per cent can evaporate. This is known as the angels' share, and the cherubs in all of the distilleries on Islay must be very happy indeed.

I had the real treat of tasting some of the older whiskies still in the keg; it was like drinking a really boozy Christmas pudding. At the end of our tour Eddie gave us more glasses of the famous drams and I declared my favourite to be the Bowmore seventeen-year-old – not quite old enough to vote, but mature enough to be glorious and golden.

Standing on the balcony overlooking Loch Indaal and watching the sun go down with a dram of seventeen-year-old malt in your hand is a moment to remember and cherish.

Jura

The sense of wildness and adventure is what attracts people to Jura, but these days the island is much more accessible. We flew from Glasgow to Islay, which takes forty minutes over some incredible scenery, then drove for just half an hour from the airport to the ferry terminal at Port Askaig to make the tiny crossing to Jura. It's just a five-minute hop, but you really feel as though you are undertaking a journey into the wild.

The ferryman taking us across smiled wryly when I asked if we would have the chance to see any red deer over in Jura. It turns out there are around five thousand wild deer on the island, vastly outnumbering the population of 180 human beings. We were thrilled to see our first deer poking her head above the hillside about two minutes out of the ferry terminal. After that, sightings became commonplace, but we never tired of seeing these beautiful creatures.

Wild and wonderful Jura, where red deer abound.

The only real village on Jura is Craighouse, where most of the population live. It has a hotel, shop and, yes, a distillery. Isle of Jura whisky is very different from the more peaty malts on Islay. It is a smooth and subtle dram that has become highly sought after. In Craighouse there's also a great little café/restaurant, aptly called Antlers in honour of the herds of deer, where you can get really good food, happy and cheerful service, and also pick up some local arts and crafts.

As well as its deer population, the island is famous for the Paps of Jura, mountains that got their name because they resemble big, peach-like breasts – although it is rather disconcerting to discover there are three of them . . . The Paps dominate any view of Jura from all directions, and they attract climbers and walkers from all over the world. As with all Scottish mountains, you need to have the correct gear and show respect. The weather can change rapidly and the temperatures can plummet. You don't want to be stranded in freezing

Time stands still on Jura.

fog without proper warm clothing and decent footwear. One of the reasons I was so keen to visit Jura was because this is where George Orwell wrote *Nineteen Eighty-Four*. When I was at school I did my sixth-year dissertation on Orwell, specifically about his writing on poverty. The ending of *Nineteen Eighty-Four* still makes me cry because of the way all hope is crushed and Winston ends up 'loving' Big Brother. It is believed Orwell thought long and hard about the title of the book, but then decided simply to reverse the last two numbers of the year of its completion, turning 1948 to 1984.

One of the reasons I was so keen to visit Jura was because this is where George Orwell wrote Nineteen Eighty-Four.

Orwell came to Jura to live and work in the summer of 1946. His wife had recently died after a botched operation and he brought their three-year-old adopted son Richard with him. He described Jura as the most 'ungettable' place, and for him that was the attraction. He wanted somewhere remote, peaceful and quiet to write his book and he stayed in a spartan cottage named Barnhill at the northern end of the island, living very simply.

While on Jura with his son and visiting family members the following year, Orwell took a boat trip to Corryvreckan, the world's third largest whirlpool, which lies to the north of the island and is extremely dangerous. They almost came a cropper when their rowing boat was sucked into its clutches, and had to be rescued by fishermen. The incident affected Orwell's already weak chest very severely, and that winter of 1947 he was diagnosed with TB and taken for treatment to Hairmyres Hospital in East Kilbride.

Orwell finished his book in December 1948, but soon after had to leave Jura because his health had become so bad. The damp climate and basic conditions must have contributed to his decline and he died in January 1950. Jura's very wildness is its main attraction. I will be back to climb the Paps, stay overnight in the cosy hotel and enjoy the hospitality of one of the most peaceful and spectacular places on earth.

Mull

Everything about Mull seems larger than life. The mountains are bigger, the castles appear grander and even the birds soaring high in the sky look impossibly huge.

On closer inspection, those big birds of prey turn out to be sea eagles, brought back from the brink of extinction thanks to a bold and forward-thinking conservation programme which began on the island of Rum in the mid-seventies. Using sea eagles brought from Scandinavia, these beautiful birds, with wingspans of over 8 feet (2.5 metres), are now firmly established along the north-west coast of Scotland. There are around thirty-three pairs of sea eagles in Scotland, with eleven of them settled on Mull. The RSPB has a site at Glen Seilisdeir on western Mull where you have a very good chance of spotting some, as well as golden eagles, hen harriers and buzzards.

Obviously wildlife is a big attraction for visitors, and Mull is a terrific base to go on boat trips to see whales (Minkie whales and orcas often make an appearance and if you are lucky will come close to the boat to say hello) and to visit Fingal's Cave on the island of Staffa, about 6 miles off the west coast of Mull, where the crashing of the waves inspired Mendelssohn's *Hebrides Overture*.

The dramatic scenery in Mull simply takes your breath away.

Mull is the second largest of the Inner Hebrides, lying off the Morvern and Ardnamurchan peninsulas of mainland Scotland, to the north of Jura and Colonsay, and easy to reach by ferry from Oban or Lochaline in Morven and Kilchoan in Ardnamurchan. I first came here when I was a kid, as a day-tripper on the ferry from Oban with my mum and dad and brother Graham, who was just a baby at the time. It only takes about forty-five minutes to cross and it's a delightful sail in the sunshine. I do remember that it rained the whole time we were there, though, but we still enjoyed ourselves and I always wanted to go back to explore even more of this beautiful island.

I eventually returned as a reporter in the eighties to do a feature on the abundant wildlife on Mull and also the notorious 'Tobermory Skull'. The story behind the 'skull' concerns the wreck in Tobermory Bay of a Spanish galleon believed to be part of the Spanish Armada, which was defeated by the staunchly brave and daring sailors of Elizabeth I in 1588. This particular stately galleon limped up the west coast trying to flee the feisty little English ships nipping at her heels, and made it all the way to the Hebrides, where the crew anchored in Tobermory, Mull's capital, to take on water and provisions.

Apparently there was some sort of dispute over payment to the locals and the ship 'somehow' caught fire. Because this was a warship carrying dynamite, there was inevitably a massive explosion, which caused her to sink to the bottom of the bay. There have been salvage operations over the years to try to recover the rumoured sunken treasure of golden doubloons, but little has been found apart from a few coins and a skull reportedly belonging to one of the Spanish crew. There is supposedly a curse on all who set eyes on this skull, but we happily filmed it in the hall of the imposing gothic Western Isles Hotel, which perches broodily above the village of Tobermory.

Of course, today chocolate-box Tobermory is well known and loved by children and their parents as the setting of the BBC children's TV series *Balamory*. In the sunshine the colourful shops, hotels and houses on the waterfront look as if they've been painted by dipping a brush into a rainbow.

We returned to Mull again with Rosie, back in 1997 when she was just three. Just like the visits during my childhood, it rained

almost every day, but we just pulled on our waterproof gear and wellies and enjoyed long walks, cups of tea and home-made cakes in cheery cafés. When the sun did shyly peek out from behind the clouds it was a real bonus, and suddenly everything looked fresh and sparkly.

If you're more of a sporty type, there's horse riding, fishing, golfing and mountain biking to be done on the island, or you can just potter about Tobermory, sit and read a book and enjoy looking out at the views.

One of the many joys of a trip to Mull is that you can pop across to the neighbouring island of Iona, off the west coast, and if you drive from Tobermory you have a chance to experience some of the scenery that makes visitors return again and again.

Colourful Tobermory surely makes for one of the cheeriest welcomes in the world.

OVERLEAF: A picturesque view across to Ben More on Mull.

Iona

It's a teeny hop across by ferry from Mull to Iona, and it is perfect for a day trip, although there are lovely, friendly places to stay if you want to enjoy this little island's relaxing atmosphere for longer.

Sailing across to Iona in Easter 2013, I was greeted by a welcoming committee of excited dolphins, who were obviously having some sort of party judging by all the leaping around, shrieking and the happy expressions on their faces. It was one of those magical moments you know you will always remember, made all the better by the skill of the ferryman who made sure we all had a perfect view of the frolics.

When you reach Iona there's the usual gorgeous white beach and clean turquoise water at the landing place, itself just a clutch of cottages, and all roads lead to the abbey. Thankfully, unlike all too many ancient Scottish places of worship, this isn't just an impressive ruin but a living, breathing religious haven.

Iona is the cradle of Christianity in Scotland. In AD 563 the Irish monk Columba landed on the island's shores and, obviously being a man of good sense, decided to stay and set up a monastery. Iona soon became an important centre for Christians all across Europe and continues to be so to this day.

During my visit to the island I learned about the remarkable Iona Community, founded in Glasgow in 1938 by George MacLeod. This was before the Second World War, when jobs were scarce and poverty was rife. George had the brilliant idea of taking unemployed, skilled young craftsmen and bringing them to Iona to help restore the medieval abbey and the monastery. It gave the men back their dignity and what they have achieved is a remarkable legacy that is still with us.

Iona is a little gem, with welcoming gift shops, good places to eat and, of course, those glorious views across to Mull.

The impressive Iona Cathedral dominates the tiny island and draws visitors from all over the world.

A Jacobite heroine

Skye will be for ever associated with Bonnie Prince Charlie, thanks to the highly romanticized story of Flora MacDonald, who helped the prince escape after the bloody defeat at Culloden in 1746 (see page 95).

Charlie fled the battlefield where so many of his men were butchered and, despite the offer of a £30,000 reward to hand him in, none of the poor, brave, impoverished Highlanders gave him up. Instead, they risked their lives, and were often killed, in helping him. After five months on the run, Charlie met Flora. She was the daughter of a tenant farmer on South Uist, but after her father's death she grew up in the house of the chief of the MacDonald clan and was educated in Edinburgh. She was back in South Uist visiting her brother when she was asked to help the prince escape and, after at first calling the plan 'fantastical', agreed. From the neighbouring island of Benbecula she took him 'over the sea to Skye' in a small boat, with the prince rather ignominiously disguised as a large Irish servant woman.

Charlie eventually fled to France and ended his days as a violent drunk, while Flora was arrested and sent to the Tower of London. She was eventually set free and went on to marry, living until the age of sixty-eight, which was a fine innings for those times. However, despite promises made to her by the prince when they reached Portree, she never saw him again.

Every time I've visited Skye I've discovered something new to enjoy, whether it's a restaurant, a castle or museum, or just another glorious view. Sporty pals have enjoyed climbing, mountain biking, kayaking and sailing on the island. Kids love the beaches, boat trips to see seals, and looking for imps and sprites in the Fairy Glen near Uig and swimming in the fairy pools.

A view of Trotternish and the famous Old Man of Storr.
OVERLEAF: The dramatic and imposing Cuillins of Skye.

Barra and Vatersay

I had always longed to visit Barra in the south of the Outer
Hebrides, ever since discovering that planes arriving on this jewel
of an island land on the beach, and that the airport's timetable is
subject to the tides. It sounded impossibly quirky and romantic.

The flight from Glasgow is just under an hour, and on a clear day
you are treated to some stunning scenery en route, followed by a
landing to remember on the pure white sands of Traigh Mhor Bay
in the north of the island. In 2011 Barra's 'runway' was voted the
world's most stunning landing spot for planes, rightly triumphing
over the Maldives and St Barts in the Caribbean. You just have to
remember that there might be a short delay if a sheep or stranded
seal needs to be rescued from the beach before you can touch down.

We came, back in 1987, like so many TV crews, to do a feature
on the famous Cocklestrand runway and also to film a piece
on Barra being on the shortlist of the most beautiful islands in
the world. There's only one real village on the island, and that's
Castlebay (Bagh a Chaisteil), named with admirable logic as there
is indeed a castle in the middle of the bay. It is called Kisimul Castle
and it is the ancestral home of the Clan MacNeil, who owned Barra

A unique landscape

The Gaelic word *machair* means a low-lying, fertile, grassy plain found only in
the Outer Hebrides and along the west coast of Ireland. The white sands of
the beaches, made up mostly of crushed sea shells, are blown on to the grass
by strong Atlantic winds. Combined with centuries of
traditional cultivation by crofters, this has resulted in rich
land that blooms with flowers and buzzes with insects
and birds during spring and summer. In the springtime
tiny blue, pink and yellow flowers carpet the *machair*,
just one of the many features that make the Outer
Hebrides so very special.

The beach runway at Barra airport makes for a memorable landing.

from 1427 until 1838. Unfortunately the MacNeils then sold the island to Colonel Gordon of Cluny, who had the frankly bonkers idea of turning the whole island into some sort of prison or penal colony. When the government wisely declined his crackpot proposal, in 1851 Cluny proceeded to boot the islanders off their own land. More than 1,500 people were forced on to ships and sent to America – even in the shameful history of the Highland Clearances (see page 96), this was an especially cruel and evil act.

The MacNeils bought back their castle in 1937 and you can visit by taking a small boat from the slipway at the bottom of Main Street. Kisimul is now run by Historic Scotland after the clan chief leased it to them for a thousand years for a pound and a bottle of whisky. The castle is more functional than picturesque, but it is all part of this island's charm.

Barra might be just four miles long and eight miles wide, but there's so much to do, and it's perfect for a short break. For a fantastic view of Castlebay and the island of Vatersay you need to climb to the top of Heaval (1,260 feet/384 metres), just to the north-east of the town and the largest hill on Barra, where a small white statue of the Madonna and child looks out to sea.

A chink of light provides a stunning view of Castlebay.

OVERLEAF: Vatersay is now a short drive across the causeway from Barra.

LORRAINE KELLY'S SCOTLAND

I managed to scamper right to the top of Heaval back in the eighties with my film crew and all our gear, but on my most recent visit a mixture of vertigo and exhaustion meant I didn't quite make it all the way. The views were still as stunning, though, and if you are lucky enough to see the rays of the sun hit the water it is simply breathtaking.

When I first visited Barra you still had to take the ferry across to Vatersay, a small island to the south that achieves the impossible by having even more beautiful beaches than Barra itself. In 1990 a causeway was built between the two islands and although the journey is no longer as exciting and picturesque for the tourists, it's far more practical for locals as it is now just a five-minute drive.

There's the tiny island of Eriskay, which is famous as the spot where Bonnie Prince Charlie first landed in Scotland back in 1745.

Back before the causeway was built, farmers from Vatersay traditionally had their cattle swim across the channel to Barra, but in 1986 Bernie, a fine specimen of prize bull, found the journey too much and sadly drowned. Although the authorities would say the causeway was built to make life easier for islanders and to encourage people to settle in Vatersay, I reckon it was Bernie the bull that really changed their minds.

On the day Steve and I drove across, we were the only people on the pure white sands of Vatersay beach, and I will never forget the sheer sense of peace and tranquillity as we stood looking across to Castlebay on Barra. It was one of those perfect days when the sky is an almost unreal-looking bright blue, and the air is crisp, fresh and tangy from the sea. I thought that if we could have guaranteed sunshine this would be the most incredible place to go on holiday, but then of course the tranquillity would be shattered by hoards of noisy tourists disturbing the birdies and annoying the dolphins.

Like everywhere I visited in the Outer Hebrides, people could not have been friendlier or more welcoming. Whether it was in the hotels, shops, restaurants or just standing in the queue for the flight or the ferries, they'd have a cheerful chat and be happy to answer the usual tourist questions.

The local lifeboat crew took us out for a sail around Barra's waters, regaling us with brilliant stories of rescues and more about the rich history of this part of the world. For example, there's the tiny island of Eriskay, just to the north of Barra off South Uist, which is famous as the spot where Bonnie Prince Charlie first landed in Scotland back in 1745. Apparently he chose to spend his first night in Scotland sitting bolt upright on a chair, as the bed was a bit too damp for the royal bottom. That was to be the least of his worries. He might be one of Scotland's 'heroes', and there's many a lament been composed in his honour, but by now Charlie has been pretty well debunked as a spoiled, drunken sop who wasn't fit to lead his brave, doomed Highlanders into battle and the crushing defeat at Culloden (see page 95).

As well as its connection with Bonnie Prince Charlie, Eriskay was also the setting for *Whisky Galore*, the famous Compton Mackenzie novel based on the true story of the SS *Politician*, which sank off

Gaelic revival

All over the Outer Hebrides, from Lewis and Harris to North Uist, Benbecula, South Uist and down to Barra and Vatersay, you will hear the musical sound of Gaelic being spoken. There may only be 60,000 Gaelic speakers but it is important that Scotland protects this vital part of its culture.

The Western Isles Council has worked hard to preserve the language and in 2008 the BBC launched the Alba channel, which airs programmes in Gaelic, including football matches. I've watched Dundee United games on the channel many times wishing I could understand the commentary.

My favourite Gaelic word is sgriob, which is the tingling of anticipation on your lips before you take a sip of whisky. Any language that has such rich, keen and apt descriptive powers must be nurtured and kept safe.

shore in 1941 in gale force winds en route to Jamaica with 264,000 bottles of fine whisky aboard. A movie of the book was partly shot in Barra, Vatersay and Eriskay using locals as extras, and you can still see the wreck of the *Politician* at low tide. Meanwhile, most of the whisky bottles mysteriously disappeared . . . Compton Mackenzie is buried in Barra in the same churchyard as the MacNeil clan near the village of Eoligarry north of the airport.

If you don't want to fly to Barra from the mainland, you can catch the ferry from Oban. It's about a five-hour sail and the sea can get a wee bit rough, but it's another option; and if you take your car you can ferry-hop up to South Uist, Benbecula and North Uist, then upwards and onwards to Harris and Lewis before heading back to the mainland. I've done this journey both ways, from Ullapool on the mainland across to Stornoway on Lewis, then south to end up in Barra, and it's been equally delightful either way.

North and South Uist are a birdwatcher's paradise, with lots of excited, starry-eyed twitchers happily spending hours watching their favourites, and warbling and chirruping about rare sightings they have been able to tick off.

Whenever I've visited Barra, I've always been incredibly lucky with the weather and always think of it as being bathed in glorious sunshine, though like all of the Outer Hebrides it can get very rough, rainy and stormy, especially in winter. But whatever the heavens throw at you, one visit is never going to be enough.

Lewis and Harris

The first time I visited Lewis and Harris, the largest of the Outer Hebrides, as a teenager, I underestimated the power of a combination of sun, fresh air and a brisk wind. I ended up getting horribly sunburned on the ferry across from Ullapool on the mainland to Stornoway on Lewis, by far the biggest town in the Western Isles.

Around six thousand people live in the safe harbour of Stornoway, and it is a busy, bustling place, but still small enough to be friendly and welcoming. When I first visited, Sunday was a day where everything, and I mean *everything*, was closed. There were no planes or ferries in and out of the islands, and no shops, restaurants, garages or pubs open. The local churches, including the strict 'Wee Free' Church of Scotland, had long decreed that as this was the Lord's day, it would be religiously observed. Returning around five years later as a reporter, covering the beginnings of a 'rebellion' by businessmen, incomers and younger islanders, I saw a slight relaxation of the rules. These days there are Sunday flights and ferries, and some shops and garages will open – but by no means all of them, so it is always worth checking, and also respecting the views of those islanders who want to observe the Sabbath in their own way.

The ancient standing stones of Callanish on Lewis.

OVERLEAF: MacLeod's Stone on Harris. On a clear day you can catch a glimpse of St Kilda from here.

You cannot come to Lewis without a visit to the standing stones of Callanish on the west coast of Lewis, just above Loch Roag. These are just as impressive as the Ring of Brodgar on Orkney (see page 170) and they are hugely atmospheric, especially when there is a mist or light drizzle by the lochside. There is a circle of fifteen stones and then four 'arms' that radiate outwards in the shape of a giant Celtic cross. The line from the north is longer than the others, and is almost like an avenue of double stones. In the middle of the circle is a giant monolith and a chambered cairn.

The people who hauled these massive stones into place between 3000 and 1500 BC were most likely trying to work out the best

The pure white sand and crystal clear turquoise water of Traigh Lar on Harris.

time to plant crops, using the moon and the stars, but there have been many theories over the years to try to explain their purpose, including that they were aliens beaming down to give the ancient people of Lewis a helping hand, or that they were giants who refused to convert to Christianity and so were turned into stone.

I love Harris.

Whenever I visit I just want to stay longer to run across one more sugar-fine sandy beach or to climb one more hill. It's hard to choose a favourite, but the beach at Seilibost on the west coast really is beyond impressive. The colours are so clear and bright, and all bathed in a magical light.

As on Lewis, there are ancient monuments on Harris, including the impressive MacLeod's Stone at Aird Nisabost in the west, believed to be about five thousand years old. It is named after the clan chief who used to rule over Harris and is a short walk from the road, over the beach and up a hill – well worth it for the view.

Harris is, of course, globally renowned as the home of Harris tweed, which has become very trendy thanks to intelligent young British designers who know a good thing when they see it and use the fabric on the runways of fashion shows in London, Milan, Paris and New York. Those cities seem very far away from the small workshops on Harris, where you can buy bales of cloth or jackets, skirts, suits and even handbags in the famous tweed.

Harris tweed is proper quality, and commercially goes way back to the mid-1800s when a clever woman, Lady Dunmore, decided to have the Murray tartan copied by Harris weavers. She clearly saw real potential in the fabric, which was already being made traditionally on Harris from sheep's wool spun and woven by hand during long winter nights. The results were impressive – comfortable, hard-wearing and adaptable. What I really love about this fabric is the way the colours and designs reflect the scenery and the ever-changing weather, from muddy browns to vibrant purples.

From Harris I began the biggest adventure of my trip – a long-awaited visit to the almost mythical island of St Kilda, just waiting on the horizon.

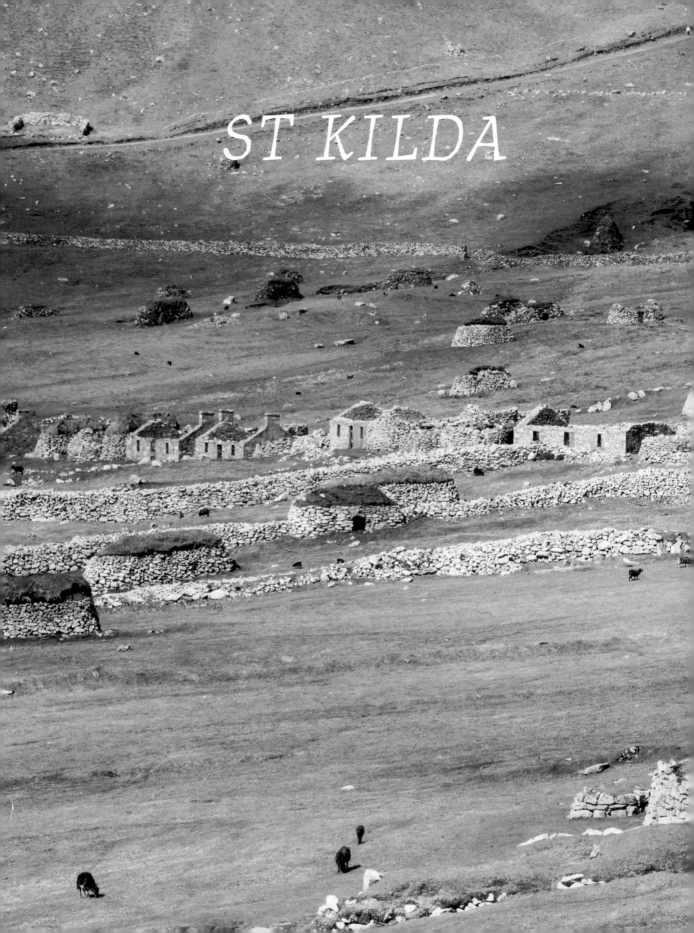

ST KILDA

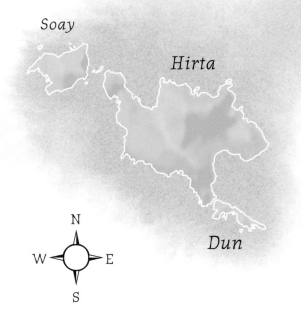
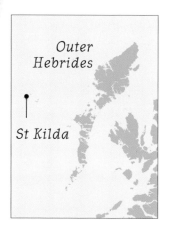

Stac an Armin

Stac Lee

Boreray

ATLANTIC
OCEAN

Soay

Hirta

Dun

N
W ● E
S

0   2 miles

Outer
Hebrides

St Kilda

ST KILDA
Islands on the edge of the world

THERE ARE SOME PARTS OF THE world that have a strong emotional pull, one that tugs at your heartstrings and simply cannot be ignored. In particular, there's a special place in Scotland that has sung to me, siren-like, ever since I became aware of its existence: St Kilda. Known as the 'islands on the edge of the world', they are a collection of soaring cliffs and sharp rocks out in the wild Atlantic Ocean, 110 miles to the north-west of the Scottish mainland, making Hirta, Dun, Soay and Boreray the most isolated group of islands in Britain.

I've yearned to visit for decades, but there's only an occasional short window of opportunity for a safe landing because of bad weather and high winds. Over the years Steve and I have had several aborted attempts called off at the last minute due to rough seas, but after a failed sailing back in the eighties I did manage to track down one of the last surviving St Kildans, Lachlan MacDonald, for an interview in 1986 and his story made me all the more eager to see St Kilda for myself.

For over two thousand years, human beings were perched on wind-blown, slippery St Kilda, almost completely isolated from the rest of civilization. At its height, the population was around 180. Lachlan, who died in 1991, was twenty-four in 1930 when he and the other thirty-five remaining inhabitants of St Kilda were finally forced to abandon their homes. Contact with the outside world had prompted more and more islanders to leave with hopes of a better life, and as the population dwindled the situation became dire. A declining population ravaged by disease meant they could no longer be self-sufficient, and starvation was a real possibility. In the end, the few bone-tired and weary remnants of the community asked to be evacuated, and the black-and-white photographs of this evacuation have long haunted me. I wanted to know their stories and what life was like for such a small group of people who were so isolated and dependent on one another.

OPPOSITE: A gathering of the daily St Kilda parliament.

BELOW: Boreray, with Stac Lee and Stac an Armin.

During our interview Lachlan spoke of an island with such a small population everyone had to work together and the needs of the many outweighed the needs of the few. Every weekday morning, the 'St Kilda parliament', made up of all the adult men, met to work out what tasks needed to be done. Every man had his say and any problems and grievances were aired and sorted out. Women had their own separate meeting and I always like to think that was where the real organizing and planning was done. Young lads had to prove their bravery by catching sea birds atop the highest cliffs in Britain. Bizarrely, after the evacuation, these phenomenally skilled rock climbers and bird harvesters were sent to work for the forestry commission on the mainland after a lifetime of living on an island with no trees. It was the usual case of heartless bureaucracy failing to take into account the needs of human beings.

The jagged cliffs of Boreray.

OVERLEAF: The houses in Village Bay are gradually being restored.

I had almost given up on ever reaching St Kilda, but finally in the late spring of 2013 conditions were perfect for a voyage from Harris. The splendid *Orca 3* was a vessel full of hopeful explorers, birdwatchers, walkers and 'island baggers' (people wanting to visit as many remote islands as they can), and even one brave family who were planning to camp out for a couple of nights. They weren't sure exactly how long they would be staying, as everything depends on the weather, and they had been warned to bring lots of supplies.

We were incredibly lucky to have chosen a day when the winds were soft and kind, and the turquoise sea deceptively calm. But if this was the sea at its calmest I don't think I would ever be able to cope with a rough passage – the two-and-a-half-hour trip was exhilarating, but I had to fix my eyes on Harris to stop feeling seasick. Our first sight of St Kilda was of a smudge on the horizon, and as well as a buzz of excitement on the boat there was also slight apprehension that we might have come all this way and still not be able actually to set foot on the main island of Hirta.

As we sailed into Village Bay we saw the tight circle of houses the people of St Kilda had called home, and tried to ignore the ugly MOD buildings in front of them. In the end it was a surprisingly easy transfer from the boat to a small craft and then to the pier, but it was easy to see that in rough weather you would have no chance at all of making a landing. How the islanders managed all year round in rowing boats is simply extraordinary.

We headed straight for the 'village' – basically a row of houses that is slowly and painstakingly being restored by the National Trust for Scotland, who are now the owners of St Kilda. The little museum inside one of the houses gives a good idea of what life was like for these hardy, self-reliant and proud people. There was no safety net. The men went bird-catching to feed their families; if they fell and were seriously injured they were likely to die. Women plucked and preserved the birds, worked the land, spun the wool of the native Soay sheep and brought up the children. Life was tough. The cemetery would have been heartbreaking, full of the small graves of babies and toddlers who died of childhood diseases, and the men and women who worked phenomenally hard and risked their lives just to scrape a living.

Their main source of food was seabirds: gannets, fulmars and puffins. All over the island there are still remnants of stone storage 'cleits' – little stone huts roofed over with a large flat stone covered with turf and earth – where their birds were left to be preserved for eating later or, under the feudal system that existed, for sending to the landlord as rent. Like the Native Americans who relied on the buffalo for all their needs, the St Kildans also made sure nothing went to waste. The birds and their eggs were used for food, their fat, turned into oil, lit lamps and their feathers made comfortable bedding. Almost as soon as they could walk, boys learned to climb the dizzying cliffs and stacks in their bare feet in order to gather eggs and hunt for birds. Interestingly the bones in the ankles of these 'bird men' became thicker than normal, and their toes were set wide apart in order to give a better grip on the dangerously slippery rocks.

During the First World War the Royal Navy built a signal station on Hirta to look out for enemy shipping and in 1918 the island came under fire from a German U-boat that surfaced in Village Bay. Seventy-two shells were fired, people were terrified and cowered up into the hills, but the only casualty was a small Soay lamb.

St Kilda remained an important military strategic outpost during and after the Second World War. One of my favourite stories, which I was told on the island and which I really hope is true, was that back in the 1950s a group of squaddies were put on to a bus and driven on to a landing craft which then sailed to St Kilda. The bus was such a tight fit on the craft that they couldn't open the doors to get out. That must have been a hellishly tempestuous sea voyage, but every one of those men was able to say they had taken the bus from Glasgow to St Kilda. Once they had recovered from seasickness, they built the MOD watching posts and buildings that are still there today. They are inevitably, as with all military installations, horribly ugly, but somehow you can block them out as you walk up the one steep, rough road to the top of Hirta for views that only a lucky few have had a chance to enjoy.

I finally have the chance to walk along the main street of the village.

OVERLEAF: Looking down at the distinctive shape of the village bay, it's easy to see that this was once a volcano.

We had trudged halfway to the top and stopped to enjoy a packed lunch when we saw the most incongruous of sights. A jeep was trundling up the hill towards us and a cheery voice called out to ask if we wanted a lift to the viewpoint to see the island of Dun in all its splendour, and then on to the summit for the chance to view the rocky island of Boreray and the mighty sea stacks Stac Lee and Stac an Armin just off its coast.

When we got to the top, I had the sense of just how remote we really were. St Kilda does indeed feel like the island on the edge of the world. It was simply astounding. I had finally made it, albeit with a little help from the man in the jeep, Lachie MacLeod, who works with the contractors that now run the MOD facility and who was a mine of information. It was a real bonus to see so much of Hirta in the short time we had on the island.

Before we headed back to Harris, we were lucky that the sea remained calm enough for us to sail to the famous rock stacks we had viewed from the top of Hirta. Seeing the sheer and impossibly high cliffs up close not only made me feel very small and insignificant, but also filled me with admiration for the human beings over the ages who had come here in their small boats and scampered up the sides to gather eggs and birds to feed themselves and their families. Stac an Armin (564 feet/172 metres) is the highest sea stack in the British Isles. Standing on the deck of the boat beside it and gazing upwards, I simply couldn't imagine how anyone could even begin to attempt to cling on to its surface for even a matter of minutes before screaming hysterically to be rescued, but back in 1727 three men and eight boys were marooned on this unforgiving jagged finger of rock for nine long months. After dropping them off at the stack to collect birds and eggs, the crew of a small rowing boat went back to Hirta and sailed right into an outbreak of smallpox. A St Kildan man visiting Harris had caught the disease there and died. His friends unwittingly brought back his infected clothes to Hirta.

Stac Lee teeming with bird life.

The outbreak decimated the population, causing ninety-four deaths; only four adults and twenty-six children survived. The sickness and death toll meant there weren't enough able-bodied men to row back and pick up those eleven poor souls, who somehow survived an ordeal that would have killed anyone not used to the tough St Kilda conditions. They lived on birds, eggs and rainwater and must have been frozen to the marrow. In a way it was a blessing. Those marooned escaped death from smallpox and so there were just enough islanders left for St Kilda to remain inhabited for another two hundred years.

Stac an Armin was also where the last British great auk was caught in 1840. This strange, large, clumsy, penguin-like bird was trapped alive and brought back to Hirta, and that same night there was a horrific storm. The islanders decided the bird had brought

Exiled to the end of the world

In the early eighteenth century St Kilda became a prison for a Scottish aristocrat. Rachel Chiesley, Lady Grange, was banished from Edinburgh to St Kilda by her husband. They had been married for twenty-five years and had nine children together, but he was unfaithful and in 1730 they were bitterly estranged. Lord Grange, a committed Jacobite, wanted her out of the way, perhaps worried she would be a danger to him by revealing his disloyalty to the British throne and accusing him of treason.

It is claimed Lady Grange threatened suicide and humiliated her husband by running through the streets of Edinburgh naked – something not even the most inebriated student would attempt in this day and age, as it gets very chilly in Scotland's capital. In 1732 Lord Grange had her kidnapped and sent to St Kilda, where she lived for eight years without hope of escape, mostly sleeping, ranting, complaining and drinking rough whisky. She could only speak English so was unable to communicate properly with the Gaelic islanders. It would have been a miserable exile. In 1740, when she was sixty-one years old, Lady Grange was taken to Skye, where she died five years later after a failed rescue attempt.

them bad luck and killed it. It was the last of its kind to be seen in our waters and just four years later the last ever great auk expired in Iceland and the species became extinct.

Despite the sad end of the great auk, St Kilda has always been renowned for its seabirds. The sheer numbers are mind-boggling, with half a million breeding birds, including sixty thousand gannets – the largest colony in the world.

It was a perfect day when we visited and enhanced the view that somehow St Kilda was a kind of utopia where everyone had their say at the daily council meetings and where life was blissfully

St Kilda is now full of ghosts, but it is one of the most unforgettable places I have ever been lucky enough to visit.

uncomplicated. But of course we weren't there during a storm, when the wind was so strong it made your ears bleed and you went deaf for weeks; or when disease rampaged through the small community, leaving death and despair; or when little children died of easily preventable childhood ailments. We weren't there when steamboats full of patronizing, curious Victorian tourists gawped at the men and women of St Kilda as though they were some sort of sub-human species to be pitied and giggled over.

Ever since that sort of contact was established with the outside world, the St Kildans' way of life was doomed. Perhaps if they had been able to cling on for another decade, the men and women could have been employed by the MOD and the island could have hung on, but in the end it was their wish to go.

St Kilda is now full of ghosts, but it is one of the most unforgettable places I have ever been lucky enough to visit.

ORKNEY

It is also full of the works of local writers, including my favourite, the late George Mackay Brown from Stromness. His novel *Greenvoe*, about the destruction of a fictional Orkney island and the loss of its traditional way of life, is always on my bedside table and I often dip into it for the sheer joy of his poetic prose.

When it comes to literature and culture, Orkney has always excelled, and during the summer the well-established international St Magnus Festival attracts visitors and top musicians and performers such as André Previn, Evelyn Glennie and Nicola Benedetti. There's also a thriving local arts and crafts industry throughout all the islands, with hand-made jewellery, pottery, knitwear, stone carvings and tapestries that draw upon the history, heritage and culture of Orkney but with a modern twist.

The islands are steeped in history that goes back to the dawn of time. The famous Skara Brae Neolithic village on the west coast of the Orkney Mainland was revealed to the world after a massive storm in the winter of 1850. To give you some idea of just how old this prehistoric settlement is, people were living, loving and laughing in its tiny stone dwellings long before the pyramids of ancient Egypt were a glimmer in the eye of the pharaohs. It is estimated to date back to 3200 BC. Experts believe that the expansion of the sand dunes that surrounded the village forced the inhabitants to abandon it – but the sand that eventually covered it completely for almost

Yesnaby Castle, smaller than the Old Man but no less impressive.

ABOVE: Rosie's first visit to Skara Brae, a Neolithic village.

OVERLEAF: The ancient Ring of Brodgar, older than Stonehenge.

four thousand years also helped preserve it, so that today eight houses, connected by passageways, survive in a remarkable state of repair and give a unique glimpse into Neolithic life in Orkney. I've spent hours looking down at these incredible dwellings, with their stone bedrooms, store cupboards and cooking areas, and admiring the hardiness of the thrawn little people who made their home here. (There's also a brilliant café on site with home-made soup and cakes, and a souvenir shop, which I'm afraid for me is a very important part of any trip to a notable historical site.)

The atmospheric Ring Of Brodgar is a stone circle that is at least 800 years older than Stonehenge.

Keep heading north from Skara Brae and you come to the Brough of Birsay. This is a small island that can only be reached by foot at low tide, so you need to get the timings right or you can end up with wet feet, or even stranded. Birsay is rich in history, as for many centuries it was the centre of religious and political power throughout Orkney. Archaeologists have discovered evidence of a Christian settlement here as early as the fifth century AD, and it is known that by the seventh century it had become a stronghold of the Picts. The remnants of the buildings we see here today, however, date from Orkney's long occupation by the Vikings. First contact between Orkney and the Norsemen probably came about through trade, but when the Vikings began to expand their territories the islands' location between the north of Scotland and Norway must have seemed the perfect foothold for launching raids on the rest of Britain. By the eighth century large numbers of Vikings had begun settling in Orkney, and within a few generations the islands had become part of the Norse kingdom; they remained Norwegian territories until the mid-thirteenth century. The original inhabitants

Walking in the footsteps of ancient Orcadians.

Sheep on the beach

The most northerly Orkney island, North Ronaldsay, is famous for its sheep, which feed on seaweed, giving the lamb a unique and delicious briny flavour. The 'sheep dyke' is a wall around the island to keep the animals off the scarce agricultural land and firmly on the beach, where they have happily adapted to chomping on seaweed.

lived alongside the newcomers, adopting their culture and language – as can be seen in Orkney place names today.

Birsay, which means 'fort island' in Norse, was where the splendidly named Thorfinn the Mighty ruled Orkney from 1014 to 1065. It is also the site of The Earl's Palace, a ruined sixteenth-century castle. It is well worth a visit and is one of the most interesting and atmospheric sites on Orkney – and that is saying something.

All of these fascinating historical places are reasonably close together and easy to reach by car or on an organized trip, and it is well worth making the effort to appreciate the history of Orkney.

In west Mainland you can also see the impressive Maeshowe, a big lump of a grassy mound by the roadside in the parish of Stenness that hides a chambered tomb more than five thousand years old. It was vandalized by Vikings back in the twelfth century and you can still see their graffiti carved into the walls of the tomb, some of which is just basically 'Thorfinn was here' – which is what people still scrawl on their school desks or in public toilets to this day.

And near Maeshowe is my very favourite ancient site. The atmospheric Ring of Brodgar is a stone circle that is at least eight hundred years older than Stonehenge. Walking around the perimeter, I always feel that the past is very close by, and there's a palpable atmosphere of serenity and calm.

No one is exactly sure what the stones represent. They could be some sort of astronomical observatory and a way of tracking time, or perhaps they were at the heart of an ancient religious ceremony. We are still trying to find out, but whatever the answer, this is certainly one of the most evocative and extraordinary places I have ever visited.

Right at the bottom of Orkney in South Ronaldsay is the Tomb of the Eagles, another top archaeological site, and one that really appeals to adventurous children. To enter the tomb you need to lie flat on a trolley and be literally wheeled through the narrow space. The tomb was discovered by accident by a local farmer in 1958 and contains the remains of around three hundred people, as well as the talons and bones of more than a dozen massive white-tailed sea eagles. (After becoming extinct in 1918, these beautiful birds of prey have been introduced back into Scotland – see page 108 – mainly on the island of Rum in the Inner Hebrides, but you rarely find them this far north any more.)

The Churchill Barriers were built when blockships, deliberately sunk, weren't enough to stop German U-boats skulking into Scapa Flow.

Fast-forwarding through the centuries to the Second World War, anyone who drives to the south of Orkney will cross over the Churchill Barriers. These were originally built to protect the British navy anchored in Scapa Flow after the sinking in 1939 of the battleship HMS *Royal Oak* by a German U-boat with the loss of 833 lives. Winston Churchill immediately ordered the building of barriers to stop any further German submarines slyly slinking into Scapa Flow. These massive blocks of concrete look as though they have been casually tossed into the sea by giants to form a causeway so that they can walk south without ever getting their feet wet.

Once the protective barriers were flattened out on top, there was a ready-made road linking the southern islands together, from Mainland via Lamb Holm, Glimps Holm and Burray, all the way to Burwick at the bottom of South Ronaldsay.

On the tiny island of Lamb Holm stands a perfect little miracle. During the Second World War, 550 Italian prisoners of war, captured in North Africa, were sent north to help build the Churchill Barriers. The homesick Italians turned two of their grim Nissen huts into a small but gloriously ornate chapel.

One of the prisoners, Domenico Chiocchetti, was a fine artist and used his skills to create beautiful paintings on the walls. Using basic tools, barbed wire and bits of old scrap metal lying around the camp, he ingeniously created something very special. The stunning depiction of the Virgin Mary at the altar was hand-painted and copied from a tiny, tattered prayer card Domenico always kept in his pocket.

The POWs of Camp 60 used concrete to create the façade, disguising the Nissen hut so that the building looked more like a church. After the war Domenico returned to finish and restore the chapel, and there's still a strong bond between Orkney and his home town of Moena in Italy. The chapel today is still a place of peace, serenity, optimism and hope for the future.

History, ancient and modern, is everywhere you turn on Orkney. That's why one visit can never be enough.

The Italian chapel on Lamb Holm, built by a prisoner of war. It's hard to believe this is the inside of a Second World War Nissen hut.

SHETLAND

For a whole year, a squad of dedicated islanders painstakingly crafts a life-sized replica of a Viking longship, and then on Up Helly Aa night they set it alight with blazing hand-held torches hurled over their heads. Every year a 'Guiser Jarl' is elected and this is a hugely prestigious honour. He is the top man in the festival and will stand aboard his glorious longship as it is dragged through the streets by his Viking squad before the vessel is sacrificed to the flames.

Back in 1989 I filmed Up Helly Aa during my days working as a reporter for TV-am. It was my first introduction to Shetland and really was a baptism of fire in the best possible way. I could tell I was in for something extra special when, earlier in the day, the helpful man from the council handed me an invitation which stated that I could enter 'the burning site'. I'd already talked to the Guiser Jarl and his squad in the morning as they prepared for their all-night marathon, and I could well imagine the reaction from TV producers in London when the splendidly attired Vikings told me they had had to send away for some of their costumes from way down south . . . in Aberdeen.

Everything is timed to perfection and meticulously organized. At exactly half past seven at night a rocket flares up into the sky. That's the signal for the men to light their paraffin-soaked torches. The band strikes up and they march and sing, proudly holding their torches aloft.

When the ship reaches the burning site there's a huge cheer, the Guiser Jarl leaps off the ship, everyone hurls their flaming torches at it and it all goes up in a massive blaze of heat and light. Then it's party time for all of the squads, dressed up in different disguises and fancy dress, and they all have a cracking time going round the halls on the island, dancing and celebrating.

LEFT: A Viking squad marching in the rain towards the burning site at Up Helly Aa.

RIGHT: The Guiser Jarl prepares to give the signal for the burning to begin.

OVERLEAF: The longship is rapidly engulfed in flames in a spectacular blaze.

My first visit to Shetland covering Up Helly Aa in 1989.

One of my most vivid Up Helly Aa memories was sitting at breakfast the morning after the night before and seeing a herd of pink elephants at the bar, drinking pints of ale and happily catching up with the gossip from the halls. I did have to do a double take, but they were simply a squad of blokes in elephant costumes rather than the result of that ill-advised half pint of Skull Splitter I had after completing our filming. Not surprisingly, the entire Wednesday after Up Helly Aa is declared a Shetland-wide holiday.

There's a lot more to this event than simply enjoying a drink and a dance, though. It's a celebration of a fiercely proud people with a rich culture and heritage. I really like their style as well as their sense of humour, and was especially tickled by T-shirts and maps on sale in Lerwick that turned the tables by depicting a full-sized Shetland with the rest of the UK dwarfed in a small (peerie) box.

Thanks to oil revenue, roads are good in Shetland and it's a straightforward drive up to the north of Mainland and across by ferry to Yell, Shetland's second-biggest island, and then to the most northerly island of Unst. If you have enough time you can easily reach the islands of Whalsay, Fetlar, Papa Stour and the Out Skerries by either ferry or plane.

The views in Shetland are stunning, the birdlife overwhelming, but just like Orkney the weather can change in an instant from sunny and almost balmy to black horizontal rain and wind that will cut you in two. In bad conditions you can bank up the fire and sit in

Far-flung isles

Fair Isle and Foula are Scotland's most remote inhabited islands.

Fair Isle, which lies roughly halfway between Shetland and Orkney, is rightly famous for the uniquely patterned knitwear produced there, and also for being an island where serious birdwatchers think they have died and gone to heaven. The island's observatory attracts birders and twitchers from all over the world who come to view the astonishing variety and number of birds who use this tiny 3-mile-wide island as a pit stop on their long migratory flights.

Fair Isle is a thriving community with a healthy population of around seventy people, a primary school, a lodge at the observatory and a clutch of B&Bs for visitors. It's also the fictional birthplace of detective Jimmy Perez, created by Anne Cleeves, whose Shetland crime novels have been turned into a TV series.

The Vikings called this island 'Fridarey', which means peace, and you will indeed find the stress oozing out of your body the longer you spend here.

Foula lies 20 miles off the west coast of Shetland. The ferry from Scalloway on Mainland takes from two and a half to three hours in often rough seas, but there is a flight from Tingwall airstrip near Lerwick (although all transport depends on the weather). When you land you will be struck by two things: the impressive wind and the incredibly high cliffs to the west of the island. Only in St Kilda (see page 139) will you find them taller and more impressive. (Foula was actually used as the location for a movie about St Kilda in 1937 by the famous British filmmakers of Powell and Pressburger. The film, called *Edge of the World*, was shot in Foula when they were refused permission to land on St Kilda.)

Foula means 'bird island' in Norse, and you will find huge numbers of hardy gulls, gannets and other sea birds bravely battling the horizontal wind and perched on the cliffs.

You are almost guaranteed to see puffins at Sumburgh Head in summer.

a snug bar until the storm passes, but apart from a rain-lashed Up Helly Aa I've always been lucky with the weather in Shetland and enjoyed some fantastic sightseeing and birdwatching when I have been back here on holiday.

Obviously you will run into the feisty but (let's be honest) rather grumpy and bad-tempered Shetland ponies. They are very cute, but don't let your guard down as they can give you a nasty nip.

Everyone wants to see puffins and one of the best viewing spots is on the south Mainland near Sumburgh airport. It's an easy walk to Sumburgh Head and on the other side of the lighthouse wall you will be treated to these glorious little birds waddling about and landing awkwardly on the steep, grassy cliff side.

You will also see guillemots, gannets, kittiwakes, fulmars, razorbills and shags, skuas and storm petrels. If you are lucky you might even catch sight of an Arctic skua or red-throated diver, and

The distinctive rocks of Dore Holm, off the north-west coast of Mainland.
OVERLEAF: The spectacular beauty of the cliffs of Esha Ness.

in the summer on the island of Fetlar, there is a chance to view the rare red-necked phalarope.

Another good place for birdwatching, and also for seeing some of the most spectacular scenery, is at the cliffs at Esha Ness on the north-west of Mainland. From these cliff tops you can see the famous Drongs and Dore Holm rock formations out at sea. Dore Holm is supposed to resemble a horse taking a drink of water. I remember doing a report here with my hair standing on end thanks to a combination of ferociously high winds and my terror at the height of the cliff face.

The winds are serious in Shetland. In 1992 at Muckle Flugga lighthouse, the most northerly point in Britain, gales of 173 miles per hour were recorded before the equipment was blown away and out to sea.

Black gold

In the heady days of Scotland's oil boom in the 1970s, Shetland was transformed by the 'black gold'. The long bay at Sullom Voe in the north of Mainland Shetland was deemed the perfect location for an oil terminal. Employment soared as the oil money gushed in. That big fat bubble might have deflated more than somewhat since, but oil is still vital to Shetland's economy.

The Shetland authorities were ahead of their time in doing their best to ensure the environmental impact of the oil and gas business would be kept to a minimum and not spoil the scenic beauty or create eyesores. Even so, the black gold has come at a cost.

As well as a serious oil spill in 1993 when the tanker MV *Braer* ran aground in bad weather, there has been tragic loss of life amongst the brave men who toil in the North Sea. Offshore workers use helicopters in the same way that we use the bus to get to work, and I will never forget reporting on the Chinook crash of 1986 which killed forty-five people. Just two of the men on board somehow managed to survive.

I also covered the Piper Alpha oil rig disaster in 1988 which caused the death of 167 men, and was the world's worst offshore oil catastrophe. I remember getting in a helicopter from Sumburgh airport the next day and flying over the blackened, twisted and still smoking wreckage. I still can't believe that anyone made it out alive.

There really is a high price paid so that we can all have the things we take for granted, like heating and lighting in our homes and cars filled with petrol.

The past is always with you in Shetland. Landing at the big, bright, busy airport in Sumburgh, you are also close to the prehistoric and Norse settlement of Jarlshof, one of our most important archaeological sites. Here you can see over 4,000 years of history in just one place. Like Skara Brae in Orkney, Jarlshof (meaning 'earl's house' in Norse) was exposed by a violent storm in the late nineteenth century.

On the journey from Sumburgh up to Lerwick you will pass Mousa Broch, the best-preserved defensive round tower in Scotland. Located on the tiny uninhabited island of Mousa off the east coast of Mainland, the broch was constructed in the Iron Age and stands 42 feet (13 metres) high with walls 16 feet (5 metres) thick. On the outskirts of Lerwick there's another broch or round tower – Clickimin Broch. And almost everywhere you turn there's evidence of a rich Viking heritage, as Shetland belonged to Norway until the fifteenth century, when the islands finally became part of Scotland.

Shetland has a thriving culture in music, the arts and storytelling that honours the past but looks forward to the future.

Shetland can be calm and serene as well as windy and wild.

Index

TRANSWORLD PUBLISHERS
61–63 Uxbridge Road, London W5 5SA
A Random House Group Company
www.transworldbooks.co.uk

First published in Great Britain
in 2014 by Bantam Press
an imprint of Transworld Publishers

All photography by Steve Smith, except for: Rector
of Dundee University, p.22, courtesy of Dave
Martin, Fotopress, Dundee; St Kilda Parliament,
p.141, George Washington Wilson, Getty Images

A CIP catalogue record for this book is available
from the British Library.

ISBN 9780593072677

Addresses for Random House Group Ltd
companies outside the UK can be found at:
www.randomhouse.co.uk The Random House
Group Ltd Reg. No. 954009

The Random House Group Limited supports the
Forest Stewardship Council® (FSC®), the leading
international forest-certification organisation.
Our books carrying the FSC label are printed
on FSC®-certified paper. FSC is the only forest-
certification scheme supported by the leading
environmental organisations, including Greenpeace.
Our paper procurement policy can be found
at www.randomhouse.co.uk/environment

Photography: Steve Smith
Design: Isobel Gillan

Typeset in Sabon
Printed and bound in Germany

2 4 6 8 10 9 7 5 3 1

Acknowledgements

We would like to thank: Alan Storrier;
Dave Murray; Dave Martin; Leisure and
Culture Dundee; *Discovery* Point Dundee;
the Barra lifeboat crew; everyone at the
Bowmore Distillery; Lachie MacLeod
on St Kilda; Robert Law from the Mills
Observatory Dundee; and Rebecca
Wright, Bella Whittington and all at
Transworld Publishers.